TUGBOATS
and an American Dream

Captain Russell G. McVay

Tugboats and an American Dream

Copyright © 2021 Captain Russell G. McVay

All rights are reserved

All rights reserved. No part of this book may be reproduced, distributed or transmitted in any form or by any means or by information or retrieval systems without written permission of the author, except for the inclusion of brief quotations in a review.

ISBN: 978-1-7333522-8-4

Published by
Big Hat Press
Lafayette, California
www.bighatpress.com

⚓

My name is Captain Russ McVay. I include the "Captain" because being one is so very much part of my rich nautical heritage. My father and his brother were tug Captains, my grandfather and his four brothers were tug Captains and my great grandfather on that side of the family was one as well.

When people ask me what kind of a book this is, I categorize it as an autobiography/adventure novel.

The autobiography part chronicles my growing up in a Tugboat Captain's family, with a Mom very strict on getting a good education. I had the pleasure of getting introduced to the business by spending time aboard tugs when only in my early teens, time enough to get me hooked. Mom's good education mandates allowed me to step up to the highest Nautical training possible at the US Merchant Marine Academy at Kings Point, NY.

Early on at the Academy is when the adventure part of this book kicks into high gear. As a 19 year old Cadet, my engineering partner and I were the first Cadets shipwrecked since World War II. On another sea voyage, an officer passed away and I was made 3rd Mate in charge of my own 8 hours per day watch, at age 20. There are several stories of sailboating adventures that also contributed to great stories to tell.

Post Academy, my employment at Moran Towing had me aboard every tug in their New York fleet working multiple tasks from ship assists to harbor construction to international deliveries of barge loads of goods. Add to that a couple of rescues in some hazardous conditions completing the full spectrum of the company's workload.

I also had the privilege of being employed at Esso on their tugs and oil barge equipment, expanding my expertise in that transportation field.

My wife and family stories are also included in this effort and especially those of my wife, without whom this story could never be complete.

The rest of this book chronicles my rise in the Corporate structure of Moran Towing, whereby this tug Captain's kid became an owner of one of the largest tugboat Companies in America.

I hope that you will enjoy this read as much as I enjoyed living it.

ACKNOWLEDGMENTS

My wife Marion provided the accurate memory for all things I wrote related to our family and the multiple moves we endured due to our career. Things went smooth at home and that made all else possible. Thank you Marion!

Lee R. Christensen provided the accurate incite into what went on at the highest levels of Moran Towing Corp.

John Mandel provided editing assistance and encouragement.

Russell S. McVay, Senior Technical Adviser.

CHAPTER 1

It's not like I sat around wishing that my life would be anything close to living an American dream…………..It just happened……………

My parents moved into a new apartment on Gelston Avenue in Bay Ridge, Brooklyn because I was born and they needed the room. It was on the ground floor and had five decent sized rooms. That was around March in 1942. They needed the room because I was the third child following my brother Don, 4 years older and my sister Edith, 2 years older.

My Dad was a tugboat Captain in New York Harbor, which despite the glamorous title, meant that he was not around most of the time. Working on tugboats as Captain was a McVay family tradition. My Dad, Harold McVay , his father George McVay and my Dad's four uncles were all Captains. My Grandfather had a very storied waterborne life. He first went to sea at age 15 as a quartermaster on Providence Steamboat's New York to Providence, Rhode Island passenger ships. In those days shortly after the turn of the century, the preferred method of travel from New York to cities "Down East" was by water. The term "Down East" dated back to the sailing vessel days. Since the predominant wind in the Northeastern part of the United States came out of the West, all year, vessels going from New York to New England ports, were mostly traveling down wind, hence, "we are going Down East."

Even though my father's annual salary at the time of my early childhood was less than $5,000.00/year, we lived pretty good lives. There was never any talk of being poor or neighbors on "support." I guess with monthly rent for our large apartment of $45/month and our used car costing less than $400.00, life was pretty good. We were even the first family in our building to have a television, a big beauty with a 9" screen. Neighbors would drop by to see this marvel. It even had an antennae that you moved around to get the best picture. Our neighborhood was made up of many Catholics, so most of us attended the Catholic school in our Parish of St. Patrick's. I was to find out later that Catholics in that part of Brooklyn identified themselves by the Parish with which they were affiliated.

Gelston Avenue between 92nd St. and 94th St. was our own neighborhood playground. Half of Gelston Avenue was a canyon of four story, walk-up apartment houses and the rest were single family homes. Depending on your age, every afternoon would find different games going on simultaneously, from stick ball to punch ball to buck, buck to skelzee and evenings with ring-a-levio. The neighbors, especially those in our apartment house, number 183, would expand those games in the summer time to father's soft ball games in the school yard of PS 104. They also had full apartment house picnics in Valley

Stream State Park. (way out on Long Island). Valley Stream was considered way out on Long Island because the speed limit on the Belt Parkway was 25 mph, so it took an hour or more to get there. Those without cars always got a ride from those who did. My memory of that part of my life was it being a happy time. That time also included in the summertime, daily trolley, then bus rides to Bay 17 in Coney Island. Many of the residents of 183 Gelston had lockers at Scoville's Baths at that Bay, as it also seemed did half the FDNY and NYPD from Brooklyn. With a lot of firemen there, we got to watch some first class handball games in the four wall court Scoville's had built. In those days almost every fire house in New York City had a four wall handball court that the firemen used to keep in shape. We kids always stayed on Bay 17 because there were always familiar faces around if a friend was needed. I think I remember getting a quarter, as did one or more friends and getting on the bus up on 5th Avenue, taking it to 86th Street, and transferring to the Coney Island bus at the stop in front of Woolworth's 5 & 10 cent store. My friends and I were 9 or 10 years old at the time. The quarter was for the 10 cent bus fare each way and the remaining nickel got us a soda to go with whatever we brought from home. Most of us boys would scavenge the waste baskets for soda bottles that we could cash in for the deposit of three cents per bottle to get enough for a $.15 Nathan's hot dog on the way home. It was great how you could fill an entire day with fun things to do while at the beach. Growing up in New York City back then presented so many things that young kids could do and be safe like this favorite of ours. We would get up early to take the one hour plus subway ride from Bay Ridge Brooklyn, through Manhattan and into the Bronx, all for $.15 each, for a day of adventure at the Bronx Zoo and then spending $.25 for admission. The Zoo was so big that it took all day to see it all. We were all 10-11 years old. Another subway ride into Manhattan gave us the Hayden Planetarium in the Museum of Natural History that featured a spectacular voyage into the heavens. After the Hayden Planetarium experience, the rest of the day was totally taken with the fabulous displays in the Museum itself. I remember vividly that the entry hallway had a 70' blue whale suspended from the ceiling.

My Dad would have to work two weeks aboard his tugboat before he got a week off, so when he did get off in the summer, my parents would plan a trip. Many of those trips were to go to my grandfather's house in Providence, RI at 302 New York Avenue. Coming from a 5 room apartment, it seemed that grandpa's house was gigantic. My Dad, an avid fisherman, introduced Don and I to striped bass fishing in the Cape Cod Canal. What an experience that was. It started with driving up to Uncle Charlie's and Aunt Lucy's house in Boston. Aunt Lucy was my Mom's sister. After a short sleep, we got up at midnight and drove an hour and a half to the Canal. We caught live bait in the herring run using nets and then we would start fishing as the sun came up. I never did catch one, but my Uncle Charlie, Dad and Don caught a few of 20 lb. stripers. It was unforgettable! When we returned to Providence, my grandfather would regale us with stories of when he worked for Arrundel Dredging Company as a tug Captain. Arrundel had dredges that dug the channels, then their tugs and dump scows took the sand out to deep water to be dumped. The biggest job he was on was helping to build the Cape Cod Canal. Grandpa was a fabulous story teller and when he would stop by our house in Brooklyn, he would always tell stories to Don, Edith and I before bedtime. They usually painted colorful pictures of trips he'd taken up the Congo River in Africa and included all the exotic animals he encountered. These were all in his vivid imagination and were so real to us. I later learned that the most exotic trips he took were up the Connecticut River. But….that was alright.

Don and I would go exploring around Providence and found Roger Williams Park in the middle of that part of town. We found that early in the morning, around daybreak, there were big fish right at the shoreline. Just for the adventure of it, Don and I decided to catch some. So, one morning, armed with baseball bats and a bucket, we ventured to the park. Using all the stealth that young kids could muster, we went down to the edge of the lake and…... whack! whack!….we had ourselves two good sized catfish. It was very important to show off our catch, so we brought them home in the bucket and not wanting them to die, we filled up the bathtub upstairs and put our fish in them. We were waiting for people to get up. All went well until……….we didn't hear Grandma get up to go to the bathroom………..blood curdling screams came from upstairs. I don't remember what the punishment was, but it must have been severe.

On another trip while in Rhode Island, we would go down to Point Judith, RI to visit our Grandpa's brother, Uncle Ira. He was also a licensed Master Mariner but now chose to be a lobsterman in the latter part of his life. When he knew the families were coming, he would put together a clambake on the beach in front of his house. He would dig a huge hole in the sand and fill it with rocks. For many hours there would be a fire going in the hole until the rocks were white hot. They would then throw a thick layer of seaweed on the rocks, then a layer of lobsters. That was followed with another layer of seaweed with a bags of clams on that. Then the last layer with corn in their husks before the final layer of seaweed. All of us kids were then told to heave buckets of sea water onto the pile, causing steam to erupt. To me, lobsters were ugly and inedible (what a jerk). My Mom loved them and was in lobster heaven. I did go home with a sword from a real swordfish that Uncle Ira had caught.

My brother Don and I did things together when we were off on trips like this. At home, his being four years older, he was in a totally different social strata than I, so we rarely did things together. It wasn't until later, when I was big enough, that we became closer and shared a lot of good memories.

CHAPTER 2

My Dad surprised us one summer by arranging with his cousin, Ernest McVay, to borrow his 35' sloop, Tango, for a cruise for our whole family. The boat was moored in Riverside, RI where we started our 5 day cruise down Narragansett Bay and out to Block Island. Spectacular weather made it a fabulous trip and just the adventure of sleeping overnight on "our" boat was a joy. Dad taught Don, Edith and I the basics of sailing and moving without the noise of a motor was great. My Mom couldn't sleep below and slept up in the cockpit in a sleeping bag. I don't think she slept much because she could tell us about the fishermen on the jetty yelling about their catches to each other. We anchored in the Old Harbor of Block Island. Our introduction to sailing was nothing but positive.

My Mom was an educated teacher when she met my Dad, but once she started to have a family she stopped working and concentrated her efforts on the family. We certainly knew that she was an ex teacher, since she demanded nothing but the best from us kids in school. As a result, Don, Edith and myself brought home report cards with the high grades she expected. I don't ever remember any of us getting in trouble of any kind during our grammar school days as Mom demanded. She was a tough, no nonsense person when it came to our behavior. I remember an incident: we were off from school on Good Friday and my friend Larry Reilly, who lived across the street, and I went crabbing down at the shore by the Belt Parkway in the morning. We did it often as a fun thing to do and we would stop at the fish market and get a couple of fish heads for bait. I was under strict orders to be back at church at noon for the Three Hours Devotion honoring the crucifixion of Jesus. Most of us Catholic students were expected to be there. Larry and I found a raft floating by the rocks at the shore and decided a Huck Finn trip was what we should do. We had a couple of boards for oars and ventured forth, actually about 200' offshore. I was to get my first lesson on how strong the currents were in The Narrows (that body of water between Brooklyn and Staten Island). The current was ebbing and heading out to sea. It took us paddling hard to keep us from heading out to sea as well and we wound up down the shore a mile or so at Bay 8th street Brooklyn. Even running at full speed, we would never be able to get back to St. Patrick's on time. So, a little after 3:00 PM, I went home and was greeted by Mom at the door: "And how was church today?" "Oh! It was OK!!!" Whack...I didn't know people could smack that hard….. "Mrs. Hudson saw you and Larry out on a raft in the river at 1:30 today."

Aside from missing the three hours devotion, I really did participate in our Church community. When old enough, I signed up to be an altar boy, following in Don's footsteps. St. Patrick's was responsible for not only all the services at the main church, but other facilities as well. Within the boundaries of St. Patrick's Parish there was also a convent of monastic nuns living in a walled community and were called the Visitation Sisters. As the new altar boy, I was required to serve Mass at the convent for a week every two months. Mass was at 6:00 AM daily (they started their day early). I would get there and have to wait for the Priest to show and I usually fell asleep waiting. One of the Nuns came out looking for me and then got me ready for mass. I did get to go behind the walls to assist when the Priest was administering the Sacraments to ailing Nuns. The land behind the walls was beautifully landscaped, like a garden. This was all when I was in the 6th grade at school.

A Priest came to visit who was assigned to the new Veteran's Memorial Hospital, built near Dyker Park Golf Course on the waterfront. (not far from my rafting expedition). He was looking for a volunteer to be the altar boy at services held at the hospital. Those included: daily Mass at 7:00 AM, Monday through Saturday and Sunday Mass at 8:00 AM. I volunteered even though it meant getting up every day at six o'clock, having a quick breakfast and then bicycling a mile to the hospital. When Mass was over, it was another bike trip home, a quick change and then off to school. This had to be done regardless of the weather which could get pretty rough at times, especially in the winter. One nice benefit though, was after every Sunday Mass, the Father would take me and a couple of hospital workers who attended Mass out to a restaurant for breakfast. I always recall those times with pleasant thoughts.

CHAPTER 3

My friend, Larry Reilly, who lived across the street, was the youngest of three brothers. His two older brothers were NYPD officers, so he was the youngest by a lot. The older brothers had set up a gym in their basement for themselves to keep in shape for the job. Larry had invited me to join him using the weights and machines and we set up a program of times where we could do it. We were pumping iron about the same time that the Charles Atlas ads were showing the muscled guy at the beach, kicking sand onto the blanket of the skinny kid. The skinny kid then started the Charles Atlas program and in short order was returning the favor to the original antagonist. We didn't have anyone bothering us, we just enjoyed it.

We did our program through the entire 7th and 8th grade years. I remember being able to snap lift 125 lbs from the floor to over my head with one arm. I could regularly beat Don's friends in arm wrestling. I did continue lifting weights for many years.

My best friend, Paul Daniti lived upstairs in the same apartment building as us. He was a little older than I but we had played together from 4 years old or so. His father was a policeman and had a locker at Scoville's Baths in Coney Island, so Paul and I really did things together during the summer. The movie *Frogmen* came out starring Richard Widmark, showing the first warriors using the ocean as cover. It involved the use of masks, fins and snorkels to provide stealth for these US Navy men. Most people were just entertained by this new phenomenon, but we were hooked. There was only one place in all of New York City where you could purchase dive equipment and it was called Richard's Aqua Lung. The store was on 42nd Street in Manhattan, west of Times Square. When I said we were hooked, both of us were drooling at the displays of masks, fins, snorkels, aqua lungs (SCUBA) and spear guns. We both bought what we could afford: a mask, snorkel and fins.

My friend Paul and my brother Don

When we showed up on the beach at Coney Island, people would stop and ask, "What is all that stuff?" That is how new this was. Once in the water we discovered a whole new world and then we were really hooked. In spite of the poor quality of the water at Coney Island in the 1950's, the water was teaming with life, including some good sized fish. The holes in the rocks of the jetties had black fish and the open water had striped bass and flounder. We went home determined to make something with which we could spear fish. Richards had inexpensive four and five pronged spearheads that we attached to broom handles. We had seen an article about Hawaiians "spearfishing" by attaching large rubber bands to the spear shaft to give it the speed needed to stick a moving fish. They called it "the Hawaiian Sling." We copied it and it worked. Both of us became very good at it and the locals liked what we did, since they bought most of the fish we caught. Two things happened: it didn't take long for the life guards to see what we were doing and had bringing weapons into the water banned, but not before we made enough to go back to Richards and buy our first real spear guns. Now we had to find better places to spear bigger and better prey. I got my brother Don involved and he loved it as well. He introduced his friends and before long we had the Bay Ridge Spearfishing Club. Having the older guys with us and their cars broadly expanded our quest for good fishing areas. The good areas included long rock breakwaters or jetties with no lifeguards to chase us. Breezy Point jetty was the first we tried, but long beach walks to get to it and then climbing a quarter mile on the rocks to get to the end where the action was, had us looking elsewhere. The two best places we found were Montauk Point at the Eastern tip of Long Island and Point Judith, RI. Montauk had crystal clear ocean water and lots of 8-10 lb blackfish on the Bay side of Point and 20+ lb stripers in a trench on the ocean side. Point Judith, RI's Harbor of Refuge sported a 3 mile long rock jetty that had all the blackfish (Tautaug in New England) you wanted. One of the club members had an outboard motor, so we rented a rowboat and motored out to the middle jetty where the big fish hung out. We sold so many fish that they paid our expenses of the trip. On those long trips we camped on the beach, or I should say they camped. Our family car was a Nash Statesman that had seats that folded down to a double bed. "The lap of luxury." Spearfishing was a sport I loved to do whenever the opportunity presented itself.

CHAPTER 4

I mentioned earlier that my father's job had a glamorous title, Tugboat Captain, but that title became more glamorous when as a 12 year boy, I was invited to join him for a two week stint aboard his tugboat. Dad worked for Red Star Towing Co. that was home based in Red Hook Brooklyn where most crew changes took place, but not always. Tugs were hopefully always busy making money and his boat, the Tug Providence, worked all over Long Island Sound, New York Harbor, the Hudson River and the Lower Bay tributaries. The work involved the towing of barges loaded with construction materials, trap rock and/or sand. It happened at this time, the Providence was just due to come off drydock having gotten a new wheel (propeller) installed. Red Star's parent company was Ira S. Bushey Corp. and they owned a shipyard as well. Additionally, Bushey owned a fleet of oil barges.

So, on my first trip, I got to see a tugboat up on drydock. They custom fit blocks on the deck of the drydock to support the tug and then they pumped water out of the walls and bottom of the dock causing it to rise. As it did so, it raised the tug as well, til the drydock deck was high and dry and the whole tug was available for repairs. The Providence looked so big sitting alongside the dock in the water, completely high and dry she was gigantic, especially to the eyes of a 12 year old.

With repairs complete, we were ready to be off on the first assignment. The Providence was what they called a "bell boat," that is, you could not control the engine directly from the pilot house. When maneuvering, the tug engineer would be stationed at the engine controls located in the upper engine room. The Captain or Mate would signal, using a bell and a gong or jingle to signal orders to the engineer as to direction and engine speed required. My Dad gave me the use of the Captain's room on the upper deck with it's single bunk. It gave me the freedom to come and go as I wanted. The crew couldn't have been nicer and it consisted of besides my Dad, a Mate, 2 engineers, 2 deckhands and a cook. I loved being in the Pilot house but my dad wanted me to get to know all the jobs aboard. He worked six hours on and six off so, so did I. The Captain's watches were 6:00 AM to noon, then 6:00 PM to midnight. The deckhands wanted me to know their job and as such, I was practicing throwing lines to ringing bits ashore. Thank heavens for lifting weights. Making fast with figure eights on the bits and taking up slack using the gypsyhead was also learned. I loved being out on the water, the smells, the motions, the sounds, I loved it all. Top that off with a good cook and this boat became a real home.

My memory is good about those times envisioning trips to the sand mine on Long Island at Northport, or another loading port for rock on the Hudson River near Poughkeepsie. If barges were empty or the discharge ports weren't ready for them, many barges were rafted on the west side of Manhattan near the Chelsea piers around 23rd street. We sometimes got orders to go pick up a barge or more at "The Market," as it was called, and could spend hours digging out the right ones before getting to tow them to their destination. Tough work on the deckhands but they were assisted by the barge crew and me. Each barge had a small "house" on the stern where the crew lived. It was mostly one man, but on some barges, families lived. It was summer when I was aboard and it was hot, no AC in those days. We had tied up two barges to the "stake boat" off Devon, CT. Stake boats were old vessel hulls heavily anchored off certain ports or locations within ports, where barges were tied up while the tug made a delivery to an unloading dock. My Dad was going to take one barges into Devon, CT and since he knew how much I loved swimming, suggested that I stay on one of the barges and go swimming while they were gone. There was a man and his wife aboard the barge and they welcomed the diversion of having a young kid aboard. They couldn't have been nicer.

I remember one morning awakening at daybreak hearing the big whistle being blown every couple of minutes. I got dressed quickly and went to the pilot house only to see that we were in thick fog and couldn't see beyond 100 feet or so. My Dad said, "Oh good, young ears." He said he was looking to hear a gong from a buoy so he could fix his position off Northport, Long Island. All the windows were open and ears were strained to hear. Young ears or not, he heard it first. Once within sight, Dad adjusted his course and in less than an hour, we were passing through the harbor entrance. I would have loved to spend the entire summer on that tug. As it was, I got to spend two weeks aboard my Dad's tug during each of my 12th, 13th and 14th summers. In my 13th year, I was actually in Long Island Sound, in the pilot house alone while towing a pair of barges, steering that tug using the compass and reading the chart to help locate aids to navigation.

I was very fascinated by all the tugs in the harbor and admired the much bigger and more plentiful tugs of companies like Moran and McAllister. My Dad told me that Moran was the best in the business but he did not want to work for them because they sent their tugs on jobs all over the oceans. "You could be docking a ship when you went to bed and wake up to find yourself on a trip to Puerto Rico." He preferred the steadiness of where he was.

My Dad suffered from a disease called osteomyelitis in his right arm. It happened when he was young and serving on a McAllister tug that was chartered to the War Shipping Department during World War II. They had stretched nets across The Narrows, the entrance to New York Harbor because the Germans would park a big submarine off the entrance to New York and that sub was capable of launching small 2 man subs that could enter the harbor and attach bombs to ships in the harbor. As I heard it, they caught them all in the nets. One snowy winter night, my Dad was climbing the outside stairs to get to the pilothouse to relieve the watch when he slipped on the icy steps and fell to the main deck severely breaking his wrist. He was taken to the Marine Hospital on Staten Island. This was a time when our ships were being torpedoed regularly, right at Ambrose lightship at the port entrance and rescued crews from those ships overflowed the Marine hospital. As a result, my Dad's wrist did not get looked at for 2 days and when they finally did set it, they set it wrong. That was followed by re-breaking the wrist and resetting it. He was actually one of the first civilians to receive penicillin, but it was not enough. Osteomyelitis was slowly deteriorated the use of his right hand and would eventually weaken his body.

An interesting side note was that a one of the owners of the tug company, J.P. McAllister, sent his own personal money home to my Mom and Dad to keep the family going during his extensive recovery. When my Dad recovered and went back to work, he and Mom set up a plan to pay Mr. McAllister back for all he loaned them. It took several years, but they did it.

CHAPTER 5

When I was in the eighth grade at St. Patrick's there came a time to select or try to get into a good high school. My brother Don got into Brooklyn Technical HS and you had to take an entrance exam to be selected to go there. My sister Edith was already attending St. Saviors HS, one of the excellent all girls Catholic High Schools in Brooklyn. I tried out for three high schools: Brooklyn Prep, St. Francis and Brooklyn Tech. I was accepted for all three, but I selected Brooklyn Tech. That my brother was already there and a senior probably was why I chose Tech plus it was one of the top three engineering high schools in the Nation. I had to take the subway, the 4th avenue local (NYC Transit) from our stop at 95th Street in Bay Ridge to Dekalb Avenue in downtown Brooklyn. It was then a good walk to the school. You couldn't miss Tech, nine stories high and a complete square city block. It had to be that big to house 6,200 students. It was also a very unique school in that there were nine different majors from which to choose. Don had picked Chemical Engineering as his major course of study. Love of drawing led me towards selecting Architectural Engineering as a major. It also offered related studies in strength of materials, industrial processes and the details of design. This was all in addition to carrying a full load of courses in the humanities. In fact one of my favorite courses outside of engineering was advanced English. The teacher was fabulous and we spent an entire semester studying the "Greek Tragedies." That was fascinating and a big help later in life doing crossword puzzles. Of course the bulk of the studies at Tech studying Architectural Engineering were about designing structures, houses, factories, retail sales buildings as well as electricity, lighting, plumbing and the like. In those days prior to calculators being available, you could always tell a "Techie" because of the slide rule case hanging from his belt.

Paul and I also got involved with my brother and his friends who formed a club called the "Bay Ridge Piston Punchers," specializing in building and flying model airplanes in the many "Meets" that sprung up in the Metropolitan New York area. The Meets had various events like team racing, jet speed racing and Combat. These all required flying planes, controlled by wires from a central point. My brother Don was an absolute ace in the Combat events using a plane he designed. Combat involved two planes in the same circle, each sporting a 2' piece of string tied to the plane on one end and to an 8' piece of crepe paper strip on the other. The idea was to be awarded points by cutting off pieces of your opponent's crepe with your propeller. Don would inevitably cut off all 8' of his opponents crepe registering a "kill" with maximum pointsand thereby win. He won a lot. My Dad even got involved, building planes while away on his two weeks aboard his tug and driving us to meets when he was home. The biggest Meet we went to, was the annual "Mirror Meet" sponsored by the New York Daily Mirror. The event would attract thousands of folks as participants and spectators to Floyd Bennett Field, a reserve airport on Jamaica Bay in Brooklyn. The paper would do a big spread on the event with lots of pictures, especially the winners and that was a thrill. We always managed to get in at least one of the pictures.

When I was in the 8th grade and a freshman in high school, we were allowed to attend the "Confraternity" dance held each Friday evening in the hall at St. Patrick's school. They would play all the latest Rock 'n' Roll music that was fun to dance, but the problem was….I did not know how to dance. So, my sister Edith and her best friend Carol Benson, in the matter of an afternoon, in our living room, taught me the fox trot for the slow tunes and the lindy hop for the fast ones. Father Lynch, a priest at St. Pat's, was the chaperone on Friday nights and during the slow dances, if a couple were embracing too close, he would glide by and say, "Leave room for the Holy Ghost in there." They provided a great way to meet people and socialize in a friendly atmosphere.

CHAPTER 6

There are those that describe handling very large pieces of machinery like airplanes, ships, big rigs and tugboats as having each hour made up of 55 minutes of calm followed by 5 minutes of sheer terror. There is not much physical activity but lots of stress. My Dad had all of the above, plus he was a smoker and he had that infection in his bones all combining to give him a massive heart attack that took his life at 44 years of age. He was a well loved man and father and his loss to us was tragic. For someone who was gone so much, he certainly made his imprint on our family. We not only missed him, but he was the main breadwinner. Mom looked for work and happily found employment at the US Army base near our home, Fort Hamilton. She became the Principal of the school they had set up for K through 3rd grade. Fortunately we lived in a rent controlled apartment, but it still meant that we all had to do things to help. Whatever money we made, all went to Mom and she would dole out what we needed to continue schooling. At one point, I had three jobs going at once. I was a stock boy in a men's clothing store, Rogers Peet in lower Manhattan, during the day. In the evening, 3 days a week, I delivered prescriptions to customers of Arida's Pharmacy on 96th Street and Third Avenue and on Saturday morning, I delivered food orders to people's homes from Hanson's Deli at 3rd Avenue and Marine Parkway. A fun thing about that Hanson's job was delivering food orders to a lot of the Brooklyn Dodgers baseball team, many of whom resided in Bay Ridge Brooklyn during the season. That was a really big deal in Brooklyn, where you went to a school and the nuns would ask us to say an extra Hail Mary to get Gil Hodges out of his batting slump. My sister babysat for Carl Furillo's kids and I got to meet Barbara Reese, Pee Wee Reese's daughter. Brooklyn was a great place to grow up, especially in 1955 when the Dodgers finally won the World Series. Euphoria!!! Monsignor Kelly closed St. Patrick's school for the day. There was dancing in the streets and parades in many neighborhoods.

About this time, we had a wonderful addition to our household. My Mom and her sister Lucy had made a promise that if both their husbands preceded them in death, that the two sisters would live together. Lucy's husband, Charlie Quinlan had passed away. She sold her house in Boston, Mass, came to Brooklyn and made a wonderful addition to our house. Don and I went to Boston to pick up her car, a 1956 Packard. Lucy's happy and loving personality was welcome even though she was a Red Sox fan.

There was an interesting nice development in my life.. I never really had a girlfriend up to this point at age 15. I mentioned the subway ride that I had to take to Tech. It happened over time, taking the same train at the same time everyday, that eventually you began to get to know other kids doing the same thing you were doing. There were several schools that required that same trip, one of them being St. Joseph's, an all girls high school only one stop passed where I got off. There were a small group of cute girls who got on at 77th street and over time we all got to be on a first name basis. There was one, Evelyn Fitzgerald, who I really began to like. She was cute and laughed easily and I was smitten. The relationship grew and we did all the things teenagers did in a budding romance to see each other beside in the subway surrounded by others. There came a time that a mutual friend was having a birthday party, so I asked Evelyn to be my date going to the party. She said yes and we fixed a time for me to pick her up at her home. The Fitzgeralds lived in a private home on 81st Street below Ridge Boulevard, a wealthy neighborhood by any standard. I later learned that Evelyn's Mom had been a widow and she remarried to Gerald Hession, but the kids names were not changed. I dressed in the best clothes I had, including a brand new sport coat that I bought at Rogers Peet where I worked. I'll never forget ringing that doorbell and when the door opened there was a man who filled the entire doorway standing there asking me what I wanted. HOLY SMOKES!!! "I came to pick up Evelyn Sir…." I was then grilled for 20 minutes by Evelyn's dad and mom and their friends, the Duffy's, all speaking with Irish brogues, asking me about my heritage and if there was enough Irish back there. I guess I passed the test because we soon left. What happened after that was that I was not to date Evelyn alone any more….her older sister Marion had to come along. Yikes!! Well Marion was tall and a beautiful girl like her sister Evelyn. A perfect match was Paul Daniti, my best friend who happened to be 6'-4" tall and unattached at the moment. We wound up double dating from then on and we all became very close friends. Evelyn and I were a couple and along with Paul and Marion we did everything together. Their older brother, Jack Fitzgerald, was dating Carol Benson, my sister's friend of teaching dancing fame. We met everyday on the subway on school days and we doubled with Paul and Marion doing things most weekends. There were many times that we tripled with Jack and Carol added. One of those times became the famous "picnic" we went to in Belmont

Lake State Park on Long Island. It was just a day of fun with the pathetic preparation for cooking our lunch to consuming the beer that Jack was old enough to purchase. We enjoyed it so much that we filmed a lot of it, the showing of which became more and more hilarious. As such, I felt like I became a fixture in the Fitz's household. Aside from Mr. and Mrs. Hession there was Uncle Tom, Gerry Hession's brother, who was a very nice man. Uncle Tom was a cargo documenter for Luckenbach Steamship Co. and an avid reader. He could often be seen sitting on the porch reading in the very chairs that we would vie for at night as our "make out" chairs. AH! To be a teen again.

We McVays managed to get by and life continued. Donald graduated from Tech and got a scholarship to continue his Chemical Engineering studies at Brooklyn Polytechnic Institute. Edith graduated from St. Savior's HS with a full scholarship to Hunter College where she pursued a degree in education. Her girlfriend Carol was right with her. As a junior in High School, my architectural engineering studies got right to the heart of the matter. We were challenged to come up with a full set of blueprints of our own design for a two story, two bedroom, one and one half baths home. It had to be complete with foundations, stud plans, joists and rafters plans, window casing design, staircase design plus details too many to list them all. We would work on it all year. At the end of junior year, it was announced who won the design contest and it was me. WOW!

What that meant was that in our Senior year, our Architectural group would actually build my design. I was to be the Supervisor of construction. What a thrill! Tech had a workshop/classroom that was approximately 100' x 120' and 3 or 4 stories high where our houses were built. We did everything from laying a foundation using concrete blocks, laying floors, erecting walls, siding, joists and rafters. We even had side projects of assembling window casings, building a staircase and front door framing. It was a class that all the participants couldn't wait to get to each week.

My class at Brooklyn Tech was the last class that would graduate in January. I started High School in January of 1956 and was to graduate in January of 1960. That meant that my senior year was split by the summer of 1959. It was brought to my attention somehow, that New York City was always on the lookout for lifeguards at its public beaches and pools. I had to go up to 53rd Street and Lexington Avenue in Manhattan to the city pool and apply. The requirements for the job included a City Lifeguard Certificate which could be achieved by taking an 11 week course at that City pool. So, once a week, I would get on the subway after school, head up to Manhattan and go through 2 to 3 hours of training in and out of the pool. After passing all their tests and receiving my Lifeguard Certificate, we were asked where we would most like to serve. Of course my selection was Coney Island, since that is where I would be anyway, working or not. We were to work 48 hours per week, 6 days at eight hours per day and as luck would have it, my request for Bay 17 was granted. It was like working at home. I remember thinking once or twice, "this is the greatest job a young guy could possibly get." I was making $72.00 per week, I worked at a beach that I knew like the back of my hand and my work clothing requirement was a bathing suit. Also the waves at Coney Island were seldom higher than two feet and I had two cute girls competing as to who could bring me the best lunch each day. My partners and I did pull a young 10 year old girl out of the water who had flipped over with a toy float around her waist. She was blue when we got her ashore. We performed artificial respiration and pumped her lungs full of oxygen, multiple bottles, before she came around. The ambulance took her away. We later heard that she recovered nicely.

A woman went into labor while sitting on her blanket on the beach. We summoned a policeman down from the Boardwalk and he had me form a perimeter around the blanket of people facing outward. Even though he said he wanted me to help him, he was prepared to do most everything. He had me prepare the twine he used to tie the umbilical cord. I had always heard the expression "Oh what a beautiful baby." That isn't true when they are just born. We heard that Mom named her Sandra or "Sandy" for short, when her husband came to the beach to thank us.

Another thing I was able to pursue was spearfishing. When the tide was going to be right, I would be at the beach by 6:30 AM. Whatever I caught, mostly striped bass, I would bring up to Scoville's Baths restaurant and they loved it. One day when I had the late shift of 10:00 AM to 6:00 PM, the tide was at tip-top high water at 6:00 PM. I got my mask and entered the unusually clean water and what I saw was wonderful. The visibility was remarkably over 100' and as I dove down, I was surrounded by hundreds of young striped bass of about 2 or 3 pounds in size. Though they kept their distance, they were not really afraid of me. What a spectacle. The summer of 1959 was unforgettable.

CHAPTER 7

That Fall was when searching for a college was pursued in earnest. The obvious choice, given my Architectural Engineering at Tech was to go to Pace University. Pace had the best reputation in the City to pursue that line of study. It was a 5 year program costing approximately $5,000 per year. With no scholarships available, that option was not going to happen and in hindsight it was for the best. The other thing that I loved was working around the water and that caused me to look at the United States Merchant Marine Academy at Kings Point, NY. Consideration for appointment required a Congressional nomination and I was fortunate enough to get a Senator's letter of nomination from Arkansas because the New York Congress people were inundated with applicants. I was advised to try a State where no one ever heard of Kings Point and landlocked Arkansas did the trick. My SAT scores and Brooklyn Tech record were well above the requirements, but all we could do was wait and hope. It happened just before Christmas that this very formal looking letter from the Academy arrived. My mother screamed with joy as did I.... "We are pleased to inform you that you have been accepted....!!!!!"

There were no idle hands at the McVay household, so I had to fill the void from January graduation to reporting time at Kings Point in July. I got a job with Consolidated Edison, the power company for New York, as a draftsman. Four years of mechanical and architectural drawing was my calling card. Larry Riley followed and we were both hired and both of us were assigned to the map division at ConEd headquarters at 4 Irving Place in Manhattan.. The company kept track of what services they provided to every home and business by having detailed maps of every street in all five boroughs of the City. Their services included electricity, gas and steam for the large buildings for heat. After a few weeks of making corrections to maps to reflect changes in services, the boss recruited Larry, myself and two other young draftsmen for a special project. All of the boroughs except for the Bronx had maps drawn to the scale of: 1 inch equals 50 feet. The Bronx, for some ancient reason, had its' maps drawn at 1 inch equals 100 feet. We were to redraw the Bronx to the conforming scale… a daunting project to say the least. It took us four months and 1100 separate drawings to bring the Bronx into conformity. There was an open area up on the 18th floor that allowed us to place all the maps together to insure that we didn't miss a street or two. By this time I was ready for July to come.

The prestige of attending a Federal Academy gets lost in your actual arrival at the Academy. I drove the 45 minutes it took from Brooklyn with Mom, Aunt Lucy, Don and Edith and I remember saying, "Am I driving to my own demise?" We were immediately separated from our families, briefly interviewed by an upper classman, and sent to a group assembled in the parking lot. We each got to pick up a package containing uniforms and were then ushered off to the barber for a 1 minute haircut. We were divided into sections that would actually last through the entire time at Kings Point. Everybody looked alike as we assembled on Barney Square and actually marched into Delano Hall for lunch. We were not to see our relatives again for eight weeks. Section and room assignments were separated by our course selection either "Deck" or "Engine." I was in section 64-287, the 64 being our graduation year and the 2 indicating my being assigned to 2nd Battalion. The 2nd was made up of 3rd Company and my 4th Company in Rogers Hall, room 4212. My room mate, Roger Dreyer, was from Bayonne, NJ which was 5 miles as the crow flies from my home in Brooklyn. He seemed like a good guy, so all was well. I had chosen the "Deckie" course where I would be trained in all ship things related to carrying cargo and getting safely from one place to another to deliver that cargo. I, of course, had visions of the future where I would become another Captain McVay just like my heritage. The first two weeks were a bit rough because we had to attend Plebe beats. It was a requirement that we learn every detail of the Academy, its history, its physical structures, the waterfront and lastly, "how tall was the flagpole out on the square?" Plebe beats consisted of us marching down to the basement of our Hall and being lined up against the wall in a "brace"..... That consisted of standing erect, chin up, chest out and arms held stiffly at your side for about 30-40 minutes. We were grilled about everything to do with the Academy and if you missed an answer, it was push-ups or sit-ups for punishment. Some Cadets didn't last through this phase and just left. My thoughts were that if anyone is still here, so will I still be here. I am not giving up! My room mate Roger decided he would change to Engineering and was switched to another section.

What happened next was after several moves, it finally settled down that my new room mate was a fellow from the Chicago area named Graham Hall. He was a very interesting guy and we hit it off immediately. He was a Christian Scientist believer, his father was a John Bircher Conservative but most importantly Graham was an accomplished sailor and had joined the sailing team. He talked me into joining him on the sailing team and it was the best thing that could have happened to me. I loved it!!! Sailing occupied 2 hours every afternoon, Monday through Friday with Regatta's practically every weekend. The upper classmen led by Bill Riddell, the team Captain and Graham were great teachers. It wasn't long before I was actually getting to participate in some races and I found that to be a great challenge and lots of fun. I also had a good touch with power boat handling, so I did a lot of towing boats and floats as needed for the team.

I grew up in a house where we rarely spoke of politics. My Mom's philosophy on that topic was "when we elected a Democrat President for two consecutive terms, then we need to elect a Republican to come in and fix the mess the Democrat left us with." So, I guess that made her a Republican. Graham came from a house that was very conservative and that was where I was leaning, so we were good. He even managed to get us two special passes to go to a Barry Goldwater rally in Madison Square Garden. That was enjoyable and educational. (GO! AuH2O)

The military life was tedious at times but overall it was a good experience for me. I found the courses I took were very interesting and realized that our entire "Plebe" year was designed to prepare us to go to sea in the second year. We studied, aside from the required humanities, navigation, cargo stowage and stability, meteorology, seamanship and boat handling. These were all very enjoyable to me.

Always looking for an opportunity to make a few dollars for spending money, I took up giving haircuts on Friday evenings. As plebes, we rarely got full weekend passes, so I was in on Fridays. My Mom sent me a complete barber's kit so I was in business. I used to get 8-12 customers at $.50 apiece each Friday evening.

Going to the regular barber cost $1.50 and usually involved waiting on line. So I earned $4.00 to $6.00 for pocket money. It happened one Friday that a new customer showed up in my room. It took me a few minutes to realize that it was the Regimental Commander, Mr. Forster: "I understand you give haircuts?"... "Yes Sir." When done, he was happy and gave me $.75 and left. WOW! A big tipper!

Saturday mornings was the formal inspection day of our rooms, uniforms and all of our gear in our lockers. Upper classmen would do the inspections and if things were not up to par, you were awarded demerits that when accumulated could lead to restrictions. The 1st Class Officers usually did the rooms of underclassmen in need of a little push to get their act together. The Company Commanders and their staff would march in a wedge formation as did the Battalion Commanders and the Regimental Commander. On that weekend, Graham and I were ready for the inspection, standing at attention by our bunks awaiting the inspectors to come. We heard from down the hall the commands: "Wedge, Left Face. Wedge forward march." Panic set in immediately. Outside our room we heard "Wedge halt. Fall out and inspect room 4424." That was us and for 10 minutes the entire Regimental staff swiped their white gloves across every surface, tore into our lockers and inspected everything. When they finally left, the Regimental Commander turned to me and winked and they were gone. Whew! He was a regular customer every month.

My first real time off was Thanksgiving vacation for four days and I was very happy to be with all my family and to see the neighbors as well. I was very proud to show off my uniform. Paul and Marion were still dating, she was working and he was in Brooklyn College. Even though Evelyn and I were no longer dating for quite some time, I made a point to go visit the Hessions, in uniform, because I knew Mr. Hession was ex-Navy. They welcomed me like a returning son and it was very nice. We also had a week at Christmas time that went pretty much the same. Relaxation and remembering civilian life were top on the list to do.

After Christmas leave when most Varsity sports were either over or hadn't begun yet, the Academy initiated Intramural games or competition between the six companies. They included sports like basketball, swimming, tennis, etc. and also included boxing. One evening, Graham and I were visited by our Company Commander, David Bess, who stated he was looking for volunteers to enter into the intramurals in boxing. He asked how much I weighed and when I answered, "I think I'm 185 lbs.," he said, "Good. Russ, you're a tough guy, lifting weights, grew up in Brooklyn, New York, so I'm sure you had to fight your way growing up." My reply was, "I was an altar boy and never had a fist fight in my life." "Oh," he said, "that's alright, I'll teach you." I was stuck and had to do it. For the next couple of weeks, aside from running as much as I could and using the speed bag, I spent an hour or more each day in the ring with my Company Commander. We were using 16 ounce gloves, so how much damage could be done. At 185 lbs. I was in the heavyweight or unlimited division. I could not believe it when the list of opponents for the first matches were posted. I was going to fight Bob Rogaski, 220 lb. Little All-American halfback on Kings Point's football team. "I'm a dead man!"

For 2 ½ minutes of the first round, we danced around and he hardly threw a punch. He did push me and my feet got tangled up and I tripped. On the way up I threw a punch that landed right on his jaw, pushing him backwards and he fell into a sitting position. He just sat there chewing on his mouth guard and I didn't like the look on his face. Ding...Ding...end of round one. When round two started, ROGO, as he was known, went through me like all those 250 lb. linemen he was so used to hitting and

I wound up on the mat twisted into the ropes. The referee came over to me asking, "Are you going to get up?" I said, "HELL NO, he's going to kill me." The ref said, "Good, stay there." Match over. Walking back to my room I realized my face was so swollen that my hat didn't fit. That evening before evening mess, Mr. Bess gave a glowing report on how I represented the Company well in a valiant effort against Bob Rogaski. I got more than one comment saying, "You must be crazy to get into the ring with Rogo."

The rest of Plebe year was pretty uneventful for me except for two things. The first was that we got to march in the inauguration parade for President John F. Kennedy. The entire Regiment were put aboard 13 buses heading for temporary quarters in the Washington Naval Yard. All was fine except that that night 11" of snow fell. Our caravan was delayed into the wee hours before we were bunked down. We got up the next morning and reported to the street where we were to commence our part in the celebration. We watched as the US Marines melted the snow on Pennsylvania Ave. with flame throwers which seemed good except the icy water from Pennsylvania Avenue then collected down on the streets where we marchers had to assemble while waiting for the signal to start. With feet resembling blocks of ice, we did make the march and it was exciting saluting the new President as we passed the dais. What an honor.

We also got to attend one of the Presidential Balls held throughout the city and I know I felt especially privileged to be there.

The second was that we had to master sailing the monomoy lifeboats, so groups of us would practice during our free time. One April day, while sailing just offshore from the Academy pier, we noticed a small sailboat that came out of Little Neck Bay towards the Academy. It was really small with three people in it, a man, woman and a child. All of a sudden, the boat flipped over and the family went into the Sound. We were close and when I saw the adults having trouble with the child, my lifeguard persona kicked in. I dove in and took the baby from Dad so he could help Mom get to our boat. I kept the boy's head out of the water and handed him up to our boat. By this time a motorboat from ashore arrived and took them ashore to waiting help. Well, this turned out to be a good publicity event for the Academy that prompted a "shout out" from WICC FM radio touting the rescue. I actually got a medal from the Lifesavers Benevolent Association and a picture with Admiral McClintock, the Superintendent.

Another thing happened before Plebe year was done. I got notification that my Dad's Union was going to award me a $1,000.00 scholarship to help with miscellaneous expenses. It was done at the annual "Tugboatmen's Ball" in New York. My Mom was over joyed because any monetary assistance was most welcome. I was proud and happy that they would be so thoughtful due to my Dad being such a good guy.. Because Kings Point was a 4 year Academy and one of those years was spent at sea, the four years of academics was accomplished in the remaining three years. That was done using the quarter system instead of semesters or tri-mesters. It also meant that we went to classes eleven months in each of those three years. So, Plebe year ended in the end of July of 1961 and I had a month off before reporting for sea duty. I chose to go to sea in the Fall so I would be back in the Spring for the major part of the sailing team season.

SUPERINTENDENT
UNITED STATES MERCHANT MARINE ACADEMY
KINGS POINT, LONG ISLAND, N.Y.

June 28, 1961

Dear Mrs. McVay:

    I thought you might like to have a copy of the Great Neck Record with Russell's picture. He undoubtedly saved Joseph's life, and I am proud that he is one of my appointees.

    His father would have been proud of this quick and brave action on the part of his son who is following in his Dad's tradition.

    Russell has received a commendation from me, and a copy has been put in his jacket, and I am recommending him to the Life Saving Benevolent Association for their consideration.

    With kindest personal regards,

                        Sincerely,

                        Gordon McLintock
                        Rear Admiral, USMS
                        Superintendent

Mrs. Mildred D. McVay
183 Gelston Avenue
Brooklyn 9, N. Y.

CHAPTER 8

That August of 1961 was a time to relax. I actually went down to Scoville Baths on Bay 17 of Coney Island in my summer white uniform. It was the biggest welcome home I'd ever received. It was my other family and it was huge. The owner, Mrs. Scoville, offered free food and drinks which turned it into a major party. One woman said to me: "If you ever showed up down on the Jersey Shore dressed like that, you'd be raped before you got in the front door." I made a note to go to the Jersey Shore soon.

The rest of the month seemed to fly by so quickly and soon I was making preparations to get my first ship. I called Kings Point's New York Shipping office to find out what ship and where do I get aboard. They informed me that I would be reporting to the SS Pioneer Muse, a United States Line, fairly new Mariner Class freighter, that was on the Far East run. My engineering counterpart was to be Henry Sala and that the ship would be located at Pier 6 in Staten Island. Having been to the Tomkinsville swimming pool in Staten Island many times, I had a reasonable idea of where she would be. I got up on Bay Street overlooking the waterfront and could see the red, white and blue stack of the Muse, but was lost how to cross the train tracks to get to her. This tall, stately looking, gray haired gentleman approached and said, "You look lost young man." I explained that I was going to that ship down there and he suggested I follow him. When we got to the gangway, I was mortified to hear the gangway watchman address him as "Captain."

Here I am the Deck Cadet, supposedly with navigation skills, who couldn't find my way to the ship. Ugh!!

I met up with Hank Sala, engine cadet, who I did not know, in the cadet quarters, one deck below the bridge. The quarters were great, two rooms with a head in between. My first job was to report to the Chief Mate. His name was William Hayes and he was the foulest mouthed human being I had ever met. He couldn't let a sentence go by without throwing in a couple of beauties. In spite of that flaw, he was a great teacher of how to successfully run a ship. I spent the rest of that first day exploring what was to become my new home for the next couple of months.

The following morning we shifted over to a pier on the Brooklyn shore. When reporting for duty at 0730, Mr. Hayes told that we were going to be loading Heinekens Beer for the Marines on Okinawa, 42,000 cases of it. "Don't let those longshoremen steal any of it."

We were loading into a reefer box, a refrigerated compartment one deck below the main deck, that wasn't totally chilled down yet. Immediately, the stevedores started asking, "How about it Mr. Mate, a couple of cases for the boys?" I was dressed in the khaki uniform of the ship's Mates. "This is thirsty work……" My orders were that none were to be given to those longshoremen. They of course knew all the tricks but I remained diligent, even while being called all the vile names one could conjure up. About 10:30, Mr. Hayes came down to inspect the progress. The hold stevedore boss said to him: "Hey…diss f***ing young guy don't give us nuttin, with us sweatin and all." Hayes then says its alright to give them a couple of cases. Outside the reefer he tells me, "You're lucky that you didn't have a pallet load dropped on your head." And here I just thought I was following orders. The next morning a Moran tug pulled alongside our bow after dropping off the Docking Pilot. There was already a Sandy Hook Pilot aboard who would guide us out to Ambrose Lightship where he would get off. My job was to maintain the "Bell Book," a separate logbook noting times and orders given to the engine room while maneuvering. I was told that in the event of an accident occurring during maneuvering, the bell book became a very important piece of evidence.

Our first Port of call was Charleston, SC. It was the first time I had been exposed to the Southern version of race relations. There were black toilets and white ones, black drinking fountains and white ones. The difference in the quality of each was disgusting. Growing up in Brooklyn, I was never exposed to any of that segregation. I recognize that the culture of the South was a great deal different and I guess seeing it for the first time left me disgusted.

We loaded cargo for the Far East in Charleston and Savannah after which we set sail for the Panama Canal. Life aboard the Muse was becoming routine and I enjoyed it. All the deck officers were very helpful, not only with celestial navigation but also the chores of watch standing at sea. Those duties along with the work with the bosun (short for Boatswain's mate) still left Hank and I plenty of time to work on our Sea Project. Hank turned out to be a really good ship mate and we worked well together.

The Panama Canal, one of the eight Wonders of the World, lived up to it's name. It was amazing to see this giant ship lift in the several locks up to Gatun Lake. They used four wires to control the ship: port and starboard and fore and aft, each attached to a "mule" or a shoreside tug. The same thing happened bringing the ship down on the Pacific side. After departing the western end of the Canal into the Pacific Ocean, Captain Williams wanted to follow a 'great circle course" to Manila in the Philippines. I did my calculations for that and mine pretty much matched the 2nd Mates. Mr. Hayes wanted to check my math, the result of which were a few friendly curse words and followed by a "not too f***ing bad cadet." He was nice that way.

What happened on the rest of the trip aboard the Muse was not good. For my English class in 3rd Class year, my teacher said that if I could write a story describing what happened, and if it was good enough to be published in the Academy's magazine, POLARIS, it would be my grade. I got an "A", so here it is:

CHAPTER 9
A Weekend with Violet

It was Saturday morning October 7, 1961 when the Radio Operator, "Sparks" warned the Captain that typhoon "Violet" was headed right for us. The SS Pioneer Muse was bound for Manila in the Philippines. Later that day, the Captain altered course in an effort to avoid this very dangerous storm, yet all day Saturday the weather continued to deteriorate, not only with wind speed increases but with rising sea heights as well. Sunday brought with it wind speeds of 70+ knots and seas crashing over the deck of this huge Mariner Class ship.

Weekends aboard ship were usually reserved for Henry and I to try to complete some of our Sea Projects for the Academy. We were rushing the work so that we would have free time once we reached the Orient. On my frequent trips up to the bridge, not only as a respite from the studying, but to take in all that was happening while trying to get through this dangerous time. I visited the Radio Room and asked him to explain the details of the General Alarm since that was one of the questions on my Sea Project. Upon completing his explanation, he stated that he doubted that I would ever hear that distress signal because it was used so infrequently.

Sunday evening saw heavy overcast skies with the consequence that it was difficult to take star sights, although occasionally a cloud would separate allowing a star to shine through. We all were manning the bridge wings with our sextants hoping to get a star sight and the Chief Officer managed to get two. The planet Jupiter and the star Vega peeked out enough for him to catch a sight to use. The rough position obtained put us sufficiently West to clear the typhoon. The course was changed to head due South, directly for Manila. That night we had a heavy following sea and the wind picked up considerably. Unknown to us, the typhoon had changed course during the night. My next work period was to be on the bridge with 2nd Mate to take stars at daybreak starting at 0530 or so. At a little after 0400, I was knocked out of my bunk hard enough to throw me into Henry's room. The sound of crunching steel was the loudest sound. Both Henry and I were hurriedly dressing when we heard the sound of the General Alarm plus all the alarms going off in the Engine Room. We grabbed our life jackets and ran to our emergency stations. The night was so dark that we were unable to see what we hit and the ship was being pounded heavily by huge waves. When I got to the bridge, the Captain told me to go up on the Flying bridge and cut the canvas off the huge searchlight. I remembered "Salty Ohara", our Seamanship instructor, saying "a seaman should always have a knife in his pocket" and boy was he right. With the search light on, we were amazed to see what we saw……..it was an island.

The Chief Officer, Mr. Hayes, ordered me to get an AB and go down into all the cargo holds and check for damage and flooding. Walking from the midship house to the No. 1 cargo hatch proved to quite an experience. Every time a wave smacked the side of the ship, we were knocked right off our feet and then drenched with sea spray. Going into the lower hold really frightened me. I had gone into them before and it never bothered me, but now, questions were racing through my mind…...what if the ship should roll over while I'm down there?…….what if were trapped by a piece of shifting cargo? Luckily, nothing like that did happen and I was able to report to the bridge that all of the hatches were dry and no cargo shifted. Captain Williams ordered me to check the stern freeboard. As I was proceeding aft, I noticed that everybody was working at their assigned tasks. The stewards were loading extra provisions into the lifeboats; some seamen were taking soundings of the water depths aft of the midships house and the electricians were rigging floodlights along the deck. It was still very dark. By the time I reached the stern, I was completely drenched with green seawater blowing across the deck. When I reported my findings to the bridge, the Captain called the engine room and ordered that #6 and #7 double bottoms back aft to be emptied of fuel oil. This had a dual effect of raising the stern and considerably calming the waters around the stern. The huge rollers still pounded the hull however, spraying oil all over the deck. Upon checking the stern again, I found that the stern had come up a few feet. At this point, I hung a box over the side, right at water level. Fuel oil was still being pumped overboard and now with the box as an indicator, I would be able more accurately see how much the stern rose. Having oil soaked decks made it next to impossible to get around on deck. After a change of clothes, I was back on the bridge and overheard that the SS President Buchannon of American President Lines was on her way to us. However, since the Carrier USS Princeton was the closest to us, the President Buchannon was called off.

    I noticed that all of the Officers were working with calm ef-

"At daybreak we could make out the outline of the island. The bow of the Muse was right up on dry land."

ficiency; there were no wasted words or motions. It seemed the everyone was under the impression that we would be pulled off the coral beach when help came. It was evident that we were not about to free ourselves under the ship's power, since we had been going full astern for nearly an hour.

As daybreak commenced, we could make out the outline of the island. The bow of the Muse was right up on dry land. The impact of hitting the hard coral at about 20 knots, had sheared the bow at the 10 foot mark, back about 30 feet.

There were natives on the island who began to gather at our site and with their help, the Chief Mate lowered himself down onto the island and was safely pulled up to dry land. With their help, we also lowered and secured a tie up heavy rope to a rock on the shore. This was going to be the basis for our Breechers Bouy rig to abandon the entire crew when so ordered.

When we hit the island, we were perpendicular to the beach. Captain Williams was afraid that the waves and the propeller turning astern would walk the stern to the left and put us in danger of broaching. We had a bearing on a tree ashore and it was obvious that the stern was moving left. The further it moved, the more the waves would hit the side of the vessel at a greater angle and cause it to move that much faster. If the Muse did turn parallel to the beach, it would definitely start to break up and maybe roll over. With these things in mind, the Captain ordered half ahead and hard left rudder. Although it did not put us back to perpendicular to the beach, it did stop the sideward motion of the ship.

The 2nd Mate, Mr. Warren Chamberlain, had calculated that our island was Kita Daito Jima, part of the Riyucan Group of islands located 250 miles southeast of Okinawa. He also calculated that we went aground about two hours before high tide. The chance of being floated off on the next high tide were remote. Also, the powerful waves continued pushing us further up on the coral. By now the bow plates were bent up to the 15 foot mark and 50 feet back from the stem.

The 3rd Mate, Mr. Joseph Anderson and myself were told to check the hatches again. Holds number one, two and three were starting to rupture and fuel oil was already a few inches deep in each hatch. After reporting this to the bridge, I went to my room to change oil soaked clothes into clean clothes once again. Henry was there and he said his orders were to pack one bag of warm clothes in case we were ordered to abandon ship. On the way back to the bridge, I noticed that the Radio Officer had tuned his short wave radio so that he was getting his answers verbally from the USS Princeton.

The crew was ordered to abandon ship off the bow. The Bosun's Chair was rigged onto the heavy line we put ashore. Man ropes and a Jacob's ladder were hanging over the bow as well. Although they were now ordered to bring only what they could wear, many of the crew brought small bundles as well. Hank was on line to go over on the chair and was working his way forward. While there, several extra large waves smacked against the hull and we could feel and hear the steel ripping below us. Up until this time, food and stores were being lowered and then the stewards and cooks were next to leave. Mr. Hayes ordered all bundles and bags left behind.

A week prior to our stranding, a Liberian flagged vessel with an entirely Greek crew had gone aground about a mile down the coast from us. The crew of the SS Sheik was actually happy to see an American ship in the same predicament as them. They knew we Americans would get rescued. They had been aground for a week, sending SOS's and no one responded. The Greek crew were helping us with the abandon ship procedure. As a man would come down in the Bosun's chair, they would grab him and before his feet hit the ground, the chair was on its way back up to pick up another. Things were proceeding too slowly for the Captain so he called the bow and ordered the crew to leave via every available means. I was ordered to leave by climbing down a man rope. It proved quite difficult to descend because the rope was pulled over at an angle and tied to a rock to avoid the surf. My pants leg kept getting caught on the rope because of the knots every two feet, so I had to let go with my legs to free them up. Mr. Hayes told me that the first time I did that, the Captain almost had heart failure. Needless to say, it felt good to be on dry land. Henry came down in the Bosun's Chair.

The Purser, who came down earlier, called me over and handed me two bags which he said contained the ship's papers and I was to guard them with my life.. Walking up the coral shoreline was dangerous and many men suffered cuts from the jagged rocks. We assisted where we could until all of the crew who were coming down were ashore. Once that happened, they started lowering bags down with our bags making it down. I had a camera in mine but had long since run out of film. The natives on the island, mostly fishermen and farmers, brought two trucks down to the scene of the disaster. When the 3rd Mate came down, he said that we should proceed in the trucks to an abandoned WWII airstrip on the Southwestern side of the island. Captain Williams kept a skeleton crew with him aboard the Muse.

We all piled into the trucks and were off to the airport. The natives told us, although communication was quite difficult, that the islanders grew sugar and were fishermen. They were quite poor living in thatched huts. We passed by the sugar plant which stood out as the only modern looking structure on the island. I used the Purser's bags as cushions as we traveled about 20 minutes, along bumpy dirt roads, finally coming to a halt in front of a group of shabby looking buildings. The driver insisted that this was where he was told to take us. Everything was in a state of confusion as we unloaded the trucks. They had brought us to what they called the hotel, although it appeared to us to be nothing more than a large room with open holes for windows. The 3rd Mate decided that we should try to speak to the ship with the emergency radio that we had brought with us. While he was busy getting things organized, I set up the radio and started by sending the ship's call letters, hoping to contact the Captain for instructions. Unfortunately, neither of us could raise the ship, so we remained at the hotel completely in the dark as to what our next move should be.

After about 2 hours a jeep came by and the driver said he was instructed to take the Mate and I back to the ship. As we came up a hill overlooking the beach, we could see the Muse and she was a sad looking sight perched up on those rocks. Everyone had left the ship now and we saw the Captain standing off alone just staring at the wreck. You could feel that the crew there with him felt very sorry for him. Later, the crew had nothing but praise for his actions during this crisis. It was he whom we had to thank for not having one injury in this accident that could have easily resulted in fatalities.

However, things still had to done!

The Radio Operator had to set up reliable communications with the Princeton to guide the Navy to our rescue. He told us that they were sending helicopters to pick up our crew and the crew of the Sheik. He filled us in on all the latest news on the way back to the hotel. The Captain and his skeleton crew were to remain on the island at least until the ship was declared a total loss. The Radio Operator remained in constant contact with the Navy ship while the crew reloaded the trucks for our trip to the air strip. Within an hour, we were all assembled and waiting for the "choppers" to arrive. Suddenly, they appeared………..eight of them. Seven men were allowed in each, with the result that our crew was widely separated. I was placed in charge of one group consisting of three of the Muses' crew and four of the Greeks off the Sheik. We were assigned to the third helicopter to land. As this was my first ride in any aircraft ever, it was really an exciting experience for me. Getting a birds eye view of the island showed that every available acre was being used to grow something. We also got an excellent view of both ships, the Sheik and the Muse, both broken in two. How sad! We flew about 30 minutes before we saw the USS Princeton pitching in the still rough ocean. The

"The next day they radioed the carrier that the Pioneer Muse was a total loss. It had broken in two."

precision flying of those pilots, landing on that moving deck was one of those "proud to be an American" moments.

Aboard the Carrier, we were treated well and me with the officers were berthed up forward. The Navy fed us a good meal and everyone started to relax somewhat. Needless to say, we all slept well after the harrowing experiences of the last day and a half. I was awakened the next morning by the 3rd Mate who informed me that the Captain and the rest of the crew were to arrive on the Princeton at 0900. They apparently had radioed that the Muse was officially declared a total loss. All the Officers were on the conning tower of the Carrier to watch the landing of the helicopters. Captain Williams looked very stately but sad as he emerged from the first aircraft. His khaki uniform and white hat were spattered with oil and he had a pistol at his side. He snappily returned the salutes that were rendered him by the Navy personnel and was escorted to the Carrier Captain on the bridge.

The next day, we were all flown to Naha Airport, the Capitol of Okinawa. It was then that I found out that those bags I "guarded with my life" for the Purser contained about $40,000, the ship's money.

Because the Union agreement for the crew stated that if the Company was to fly crew members for whatever cause, they had to fly 1st Class, we were stuck on Okinawa for 6 days until they could get a chartered plane to accommodate everyone. It seemed strange to return to New York in 20 hours, when it had taken almost a month to get to the scene of the accident. Henry and I both agreed: "What a way to start our sea year."

Cadets McVay and Sala describe to Admiral McLintock their shipwreck experience.

CHAPTER 10

In the article I wrote, I breezed over the time we spent in Okinawa waiting for the chartered aircraft to return us to New York. We were there for a few days waiting. Navy buses brought us to various hotels with rooms available to house the entire crew. The Officers were brought to the Kokosai Kanko Hotel in Naha, the capitol city. We were greeted at the door by an American who introduced himself as the owner. Turns out, he was a Massachusetts Maritime College graduate who came to Okinawa on a ship, met a local woman, fell in love and never left. He said they owned this hotel and three nightclubs, so we were a little taken aback when he opened his jacket and asked "you want to buy a watch?" He had about 20 watches hanging in his jacket lining. In any event, it was a nice hotel and dinner was great in their restaurant. He then arranged for car services to take us to one of his nightclubs where "shipwrecked and survived" was the theme. At 19, I was the youngest one there and it didn't take long for me to be hammered. Someone got me back to my room and I knew nothing until waking up the next morning. I never felt so bad and swore off booze for the rest of my life. The hotel owner took one look at me the next morning and advised me to go across the street to the Turkish Baths??? (In Okinawa). I took his advice and was met at the door by a little Okinawan woman who took me inside. She stripped me down to just wearing a towel then she locked me in a small box….a steam box. After 30 minutes of sweating, it was out of the box and up onto a table where she proceeded to scrape off the top layer of my skin. I swear she used a rasp. Back in the box after that for another half hour of sweating. Back on the table for me where she jumped up on the table and proceeded to walk down my spine with her little bare feet. I'm nineteen and joints were cracking. The finishing touch was a complete massage using oils of some kind. It was 12:30 PM when I got back to my room, where I stripped down and collapsed into bed. To my amazement, I didn't wake until 8:00 AM the next day. Never again…..

The whole crew of the Muse was aboard the chartered plane that was to fly us from Okinawa to Tokyo, to Anchorage, Alaska then on to New York. The stewardesses ran out of those little drink bottles by Anchorage and had to reload. When we got to the private terminal for charters at Idewild Airport, there was Jack Fitzgerald waiting to give me a lift home to Brooklyn.

Hank and I had a shipping experience, thankfully, like no other Cadets at Kings Point. We were the first Cadets shipwrecked since World War II.

The Shipping Officer told Hank and I that we were to report to the Academy in two days. We had to meet with Admiral McLintock first where we had to tell him all about our trip and have a few pictures taken with him holding life jackets because we were the "survivors." I reminded the Admiral that this was the second time I've had my picture taken with him. From meeting with him, we had to pick up complete new sets of uniforms and another Sea Project because we'd be shipping out pretty quickly.

And quickly it was, since the call came that we were to report to the Farrell Line ship, the SS African Crescent. She was a C-3 freighter with the capacity to carry up to 12 passengers. Twelve was the magic number since any more than 12 passengers would require a doctor to be aboard. The Crescent was located at the Farrell Line Pier in Gowanus, Brooklyn, Pier 31st Street which was good for me since I lived a mere 30 minutes away. It was actually shorter since Jack Fitzgerald drove me there. The intended voyage was called an "express run" to West Africa. We steamed directly to Point Noir in French Equatorial Africa. Enroute, we were told that we were to pick up a load of Palm Oil. Tanks had to be chipped and scraped of all loose rust in the double bottom and it presented an opportunity for me to earn OT pay. Cadets do not normally get that opportunity to earn the extra money. I remember that at the beginning of the trip, the Captain told me to give malaria shots to the entire crew. I had never done anything like that before, but I figured, what the heck, I'll give it go. I remember when the fifth crew member came before me, I had a very difficult time getting the needle into to his arm. He was a skinny oriental guy and I mentioned to Hank Sala that he had very tough skin. Hank replied "Russ, I think you are supposed to change needles after each injection" It went much smoother after that.

All of that was put on hold, when the African Crescent ran into an Atlantic hurricane a few days out of New York. (This was before Satellite weather forecasts were available.). I was beginning to think that I was bringing bad luck with me. Two trips, one Typhoon and one Hurricane. At least there was no grounding on this one. After Point Noir, the next port of call was Matadi in the Belgium Congo and required a lengthy trip up the Congo River. I couldn't help remembering my grandfather's description of his imaginary trips up that waterway. Fully expecting to see Hippos and giraffes along the bank, I was disappointed that the

Congo River was more like a trip on the upper sections of Hudson River. Very strong currents made mooring in Matadi quite a feat of ship handling and was a good learning experience. Before arrival in Matadi, I developed a severe infected throat, so a doctor was ordered. I could swear that the doctor who came aboard was really a witch doctor of sorts. He chanted the entire time he was with me. When asked why he proscribed suppositories for a sore throat, he said "we must attack this infection from both ends." When he left, the Chief Mate opened the emergency Medical Supply and started me on antibiotics immediately. I was cured in 2-3 days!

After Matadi we stopped in two ports in Angola, Luanda and Lobito. We sensed that Captain was determined to get the cargo off quickly because he hinted that he wanted to be back in New York before Christmas. In fact the final piece of cargo to be discharged in Lobito was a 40 ton steamshovel. When told that a pier was not going to be available for a couple of days, he ordered a barge to be brought alongside while we slow circled the port. Once the shovel was on the barge, we were out of there, heading for New York. The whole trip was made in warm sea temperatures until we left the Gulf Stream and entered New York harbor on Christmas Eve morning. It was snowing. It was also great to be home for Christmas but I could not get warm for several weeks or more. Thus ended my first half year at sea and I now moved into the 2nd half of my 3rd Class (Sophomore) year.

As an "Upper Classman" now, we were finished with the rigidity of behavior required of Plebes. The regimentation was still there, with inspections and parades and fixed times for leaves and even though upper classmen got more weekend leaves, that didn't affect me as a member of the sailing team. I pushed myself more and more into the art of sailing and doing what was best for our team to win regattas.

That Spring of 1962 just seemed to fly by which was understandable with Sailing Team practice Monday through Friday and Regattas every weekend. We traveled a great deal to race against other colleges on their home turf. An arch rival was the U.S. Naval Academy in Annapolis because of each school's nautical prowess. We marveled at the extensive facilities available on their waterfront compared to our much smaller and less well funded facilities at Kings Point. That, however, did not prevent us from having winning records against them, a fact that did not make them happy. One racing weekend in Annapolis happened to coincide with the "Maryland Nursing Student Convention" held in a hotel outside the gate in Annapolis. Kings Pointer's, true to form, were the first to arrive at that hotel when racing was completed for the day. Our uniforms were almost identical, so "who's to know"? We dominated the nurse's attention for several hours until the Navy football team showed up to persuade us that only the "Middies" were invited to join the nurse's, not us Merchant Marine bums. So much for our being a fellow Federal Academy. We did manage to get a trophy though, a big banner that read: "Maryland Nursing Students Convention." That banner flew down at our pier for the rest of the year, especially when "the Middies" came to race at our home base.

The biggest memory of that spring was being invited to be my best friend's "Best Man" who was finally marrying Marion Fitzgerald in June of 1962. I managed, with the help of Marion's Dad, who had a friend, who had a friend, etc. to get a long weekend pass. That allowed me to participate in the rehearsal dinner on Friday and of course, the wedding on Saturday. Evelyn Fitzgerald was the Maid of Honor and Jack Fitzgerald and his wife Carol were also participants. It was a fun affair with all our friends from Gelston Avenue and all our friends on the Hession/Fitzgerald side.

That was in June and shortly thereafter, we had our summer leave. I had previously written an article on how I spent the summer of 1962, so here it is in Chapter 11.

CHAPTER 11

The United States Merchant Marine Academy at Kings Point, NY had a highly rated Sailing Team racing Interclubs as part of the Middle Atlantic Intercollegiate Sailing Association (MAISA). I got introduced to the team by my room mate Graham Hall who was an outstanding sailor before he got to the Academy. My father had taken our family sailing several times, so I knew the basics.

Graham and the upper class members were great teachers and I caught on fairly quickly. It was a fantastic piece of luck because I loved it. Sailing at the Academy was a three season sport with the MAISA (Middle Atlantic Intercollegiate Sailing Assoc.) races in the Fall and Spring and we went "frostbiting" in the winter against local Yacht Clubs. We sailed every day for two hours, Monday through Friday and then had regattas every weekend. Our competitors were: the US Coast Guard Academy, NY State Maritime, Princeton University, the US Naval Academy, Yale University and the US Military Academy. We would also race against the New England Intercollegiate Sailing Association facing schools like Harvard, MIT, University of Rhode Island and Boston College.

Our sailing adventure actually started in our 2nd year at the Academy. Being down on the waterfront everyday, we became very aware of the goings on with the waterfront crew. It came to our attention that the government was looking to replace the 26 foot double ended lifeboats that were used in the training of the Cadets in boat handling. These vessels were old and leaky and ready to be sold at auction. What was nice about them was that they were equipped with a steel centerboard that could be lowered when you put the "Monomoys" into the sailing mode. The seed had been planted.

Graham and myself, were both "Deck Officer trainees and Bob Lindmark was an Engineering Officer trainee were both classmates and fast friends. We hatched a plan to put in a bid to buy one of the boats, fix it up and set sail in August throughout Long Island Sound, Rhode Island and Massachusetts. We procured the necessary bid documents then the strategizing began as to what our bid would be. None of us had much money so we started saying let's just throw in a bid for $50.00. As we thought about that we determined that someone may follow that line of thought, so we raised it to $51.00. This went back and forth until we finalized what our offer would be. We would try $56.50 and that was final.

It turns out that no one else made a bid, so we owned a 26' sailing vessel that cost us $56.50. Now we had to get it seaworthy. The fact that our new vessel did not have a cabin, did not bother us. We were going to rough it but…. hoped it wouldn't rain for the upcoming month.

The dock crew was kind enough to put our boat on a cradle on the dock. We purchased caulking rope and proceeded to do the tedious work of caulking between each seam of the planks used in construction. The boat came with a mast and two sails, the main and the jib. The sail rig for the monomoys was called a "Sliding Gunter Rig." The top of the main sail had a boom as did the bottom. When the halyard pulled the sail up, the upper boom stood straight up adding another ten feet to the height of the mast and main sail. Two oars and the rudder rounded out the equipment that came with the boat. After a fresh coat of paint, she was ready to go into the water. We painted the hull white, the gunnels bright red and the interior with battleship gray paint.

The next problem to be solved is where are we going to put it while waiting for our leave to start toward the end of July. Just to the east of the Academy was the Kings Point Town Park and Marina. It wasn't easy to convince the Town government people that we really were residents of the Town of Kings Point, but we did. They agreed to let us put a mooring down for our boat. We just happened to find an old rusty 80 lb., mushroom anchor in amongst junk lying around on the pier. Since we had access to our motorized vessels, it was no problem to load our mooring gear on one, run around Steppingstone Light to the Marina and plant our mooring right where they said to put it. Before launching her, we crashed a bottle of champagne across her bow and christened her in the name of "Gretel", the Australian challenger for the America's Cup. Those races were to take place in September in Newport, RI where the American challengers were currently vying for privilege of representing our Country. After the launching, we stepped her mast, rigged canvas where we could (this boat had no cabin) and we towed her around to be placed on our mooring. At least once a week we had to go to her with a bilge pump to pump out rainwater and for some reason there was water in it even when it didn't rain. Oh well!! We used the remainder of the time utilizing our marlinspike skills to patch the sails and splice all the lines we would need for our intended voyage.

In the weeks before departure we were assembling all the gear we would need for the intended 30 day trip "down East." As far as clothing, pants for those chilly days, foul weather gear, several bathing suits and shirts, sweat shirts and hats and sneakers. I made a trip home to Brooklyn to retrieve my spearfishing gear to help with the cost of food. I also had a good pair of binoculars that would come in handy. Waterproof sleeping bags were a must. I fortunately owned a waterproof duffel bag that fit everything of mine. The waterfront crew loaned us a WWII box compass that actually worked quite well along with battery powered running lights for night sailing. A six volt waterproof search light rounded out our needs. I don't want to forget Graham bringing his skull and crossbones pirate flag just in case we needed it.

Well, the day had finally come. We commandeered a motor boat and towed Gretel back to the Academy, where we loaded and carefully stowed our gear aboard her. The dock crew and several others were there wishing us Bon Voyage and we were off. The western part of Long Island Sound did not interest us so much and we wanted to get further East, the sooner the better. We decided to sail all night and as such we divided the night into three watches at the helm. As usual in that area the wind died down with the setting sun so sailing in light airs was easy and could be handled alone. Graham and I being Deckies, we were already well schooled in chart navigation, so while Bob was on watch, he fortunately woke us and there he sat with the chart on his lap and flashlight illuminating it and asked "what do these little stars on the chart mean?" OMG, those are rocks!!! We all quickly jibed the main sail and headed North to get out to clear the lighted buoy marking the end of the rocky shoal. Phew!! We were at Eatons Neck, LI.

For the next two days, the wind was steady, the seas were relatively calm and we sailed close to the Connecticut shore. On the morning of the 3rd day, we found ourselves near Fishers Island. There was an old dock in a small cove that we tied up to and welcomed going exploring and stretching our legs. There were very large homes on the Island but we never saw anyone. We had lunch and were off right after noon. We had discovered that when we went into supermarkets, we would go to the Deli section. When loafs of meats got too small to slice, they would throw the "end cuts" into bags. The Deli manager sold us bags of end cuts for $1.00/lb. Ten bucks for ten pounds of meat and we had lunches for a week.

Our next adventure found us sailing East through Fishers Island Sound toward Watch Hill, RI. Just inside of Watch Hill there was an entry to small river called Pawcatuck Breach. We decided we would see what was there and found a low bridge spanning the creek, so we had to unstep our mast and row. About ¾ of a mile in, we went by a house, backed up to the river where a family was in their back yard having a barbeque. After spotting us, they all got up and waved us in to join them. They wanted to hear our story. What a wonderful family they were and to our surprise, the Dad was an early graduate of Kings Point in WWII. We dined on hamburgers, hot dogs, salads and desserts. As nightfall came and the weather was taking a turn for the worse, we were invited to spend the night in their garage and thus we avoided having to sleep aboard in the rain. The next morning, we were invited in for pancakes. The mother of the house said she has never cooked that many pancakes in her life.

According to tide books, the current raced through the narrow cut at the East end of Fisher Island at 3 to 4 knots. We therefore had to wait til just after high water to catch the favorable ebb current which stayed with us to our next destination, the Harbor of Refuge at Point Judith, RI. This was my favorite place for spearfishing.

And now here we are aboard the Gretel waiting for 2 hours before high water, where experience taught me that's when the fish are out and about. I always loved getting a fish on the first dive and this beautiful 6 lb Blackfish (Tautaug in New England) obliged me. I caught several fish. Graham and Bob gave it a try, but it was their first time. When we had enough, we heaved anchor and sailed through the cut of the huge 3 mile long stone breakwater that made Point Judith a "Harbor of Refuge." To the right of the actual entrance to the harbor, there was a beach. At the back of the beach there were barbeque pits and that was where we were going to cook our fish. When we came ashore, there were three girls in bathing suits, our age, on a blanket. Graham went right over to them and sat next to one girl, Bob was next leaving me with number three. She asked me where I was from and I replied from Brooklyn, NY and I also said "I think I may have some relatives who live around here." She asked me for my name and I replied: Russ McVay. She stuck out her hand to shake and said "Hi! I'm Barbara McVay. We were cousins. After a few minutes, she said her mother has got to see me. They lived about eight houses up from the beach. When I walked through the front door, her mother looked at me and said "my God! You have got to be Harold's son." Harold is my Dad's name and this was my Aunt Helen. Needless to say, we didn't have to cook the fish in a pit. During the day, various relatives of mine stopped by to see the cousin who just sailed into the harbor.

We all agreed that the next port of call would be Newport, RI. With a decent breeze it was going to be a half day sail so, shortly after noon we sailed into the America's Cup sailing capital. After scouting for places to tie up, we boldly decided to go right into Newport shipyard. We went to the head of the dock and tied up behind the 12 meter challenger named Columbia. Once we were all fast, an elderly man approached and asked permission to step aboard. He laughed at our naming our boat after Gretel and he wanted to know all about our trip. It turns out he was the owner of Columbia. His name was Cornelius Sheilds and had a seat on the NY Stock Exchange. His son, Glit Sheilds was skippering Columbia and he asked if we would like to help out on the 35' motor boat used to change sails if the wind velocity changed. We got a ring side seat to watch a 12 meter race. What a great day! Mr. Sheilds asked for our names and contact numbers and gave us his number "just in case you boys need something."

Later that day we gathered up our dirty clothes and headed ashore looking for a laundromat. We found one and it had these giant washing machines so we decided to do everything all at once. We even started taking off our shirts to throw them in as well. There were women there waiting for their clothes to finish. They started clapping and chanting "take it off, take it all off." We didn't oblige them but we had a good laugh with them. Enroute to the laundromat we passed a Howard Johnson restaurant that was advertising "Fried chicken, All you can eat for $4.99." By the time we were done, I am sure that they will second guess doing that deal again. Get 3 pieces, put one in our bag and then get 3 more pieces. We had chicken for the next few days.

That night, while still at Newport Shipyard, it began to rain. Across the dock from Gretel was an unlocked sail locker. We grabbed our sleeping bags and moved over to the locker and slept on bagged sails and kept dry. At about midnight, a man with a flashlight comes in yelling at us… "I'm the sheriff of this county and you boys have 24 hours to get out of town." We had all we could do to muffle our laughter. We told him we would be leaving early the next morning and he left.

Our departure from Newport was highlighted by our meeting the USN Destroyer "The Five Sullivans", so named for a family who lost five sons on D Day or shortly thereafter.

Graham decided to salute them by running our pirate flag up the mast. We saw lots of activity on the bridge of the ship with a sailor dispatched to their flag halyard who then ran up their Irish flag. We each dipped our flags as a salute and the ship finished it with blast of their horn. Great fun.

Despite fog setting in, we headed for Cuttyhunk Island, part of the Elizabeth Island group, navigating across the entrance to Buzzards Bay going from buoy to buoy. Out of the fog came a 54' Chris Craft Commander that we could hear before we saw it. The skipper of that power boat came up close to us and yelled "which way to Point Judith?'

Unbelievable!!! We asked"do you have a chart?", which he replied showing us a Texaco Oil cruise map. We pointed in the general direction and off they went. Scary that someone of so little common sense was out on the water.

Cuttyhunk was uneventful other than it was on Sunday and the weekend cruisers were heading home. A couple of them asked if we would like some food, that they didn't want to carry home. All gifts gratefully received. We should have that printed on the side of our boat. We departed Cuttyhunk heading Southeast to run along the south shore of Martha's Vinyard. We stopped in Edgartown Great Pond, a salt water lake, on which one of our instructors at the Academy had a summer vacation home. He and his wife were happy to see us and we stayed two nights. An interesting aside was that they had next door neighbors who were very different. The husband was 7'-4" tall, the wife was 6'-10" and their son was 7'-2" and they had constructed their house to reflect their size. Doorways were 9' tall, and sinks were on 44" countertops. While visiting them, I had asked to use the bathroom and when I sat down, my feet were 6" off the floor. I felt like I was 5 years old.

From Martha's Vineyard we decided it was time to turn our bow to the West and head home. It turned out that it was not going to be easy to buck the wind for the 100+ mile journey back to Kings Point. We made it easily to Halletts Point on the North fork of the end of Long Island. We then sailed close hauled into the Westerly wind from Halletts Point all the way over to Connecticut where we tacked and sailed all the back to Long Island winding up right back at Halletts Point. We made no progress. We dropped the hook close to shore and waded ashore. There was a set of stairs going up the side of the cliff so we decided to see what was up there. Turned out to be a summer vacation spot for families who bought or rented cabins. Everyone was super friendly and even invited to participate in a soft ball game where they needed a couple more players. When they looked down at our boat anchored below, they could not believe where we had been.

We took off early the next day in light airs but a favorable current. A little history here…… my father was a tugboat Captain and when I was 12 to 14 years old, he would take me with him for two weeks at a time to live on his tug. I got a first hand lesson in navigation, tides and currents and I became very much aware of the work done by tugboats and how they do it. So, on this morning, when we were halfway across Long Island Sound, I looked East and spotted a Great Lakes Dredge and Drydock tug towing two large dump scows heading Westbound towards New York. An idea was sprung. We broke out our anchor line and got the end of it not attached to the anchor and tied a bowline knot forming big loop. We maneuvered ourselves to be right up close to the side of the second scow moving at about 4 knots…. This was going to be a one shot deal…..and as the stern was approaching, I heaved the line and the loop rung the stern bit on the scow just like I practiced when riding on the Providence with my Dad. We let out about 50' of line and then made it fast to the base of our mast. Again, we set up watches to man the rudder and keep Gretel following directly behind the scow. I don't know whether the tug crew knew we were there, but they really couldn't do anything about it. We also didn't know how far the tug was going. Turned out he was going all the way to New York. After 18-20 hours of being towed, we were abeam of Steppingstone Lighthouse near Kings Point. We raised the sails, centerboard down, then we cut the towline. We sailed into the Academy, secured the boat and went to sleep, since it was the middle of the night. The next day we were greeted by the dock crew and regaled them with the story of our adventures. They were so helpful, finding a place for us to stow the boat and gear for the winter.

How lucky can you be to have three guys who were so compatible that we could spend 30 days of roughing it without a complaint. There was no Captain of this boat, if something needed to be done it was done without talking about it. We knew this was an adventure we'd never forget but we each had to get home to pack up to go to sea for the second half of our sea year aboard ship. We would be on ships until we reported back to the Academy after New Years.

CHAPTER 12

The third year at the U.S. Merchant Marine Academy was divided into two sections. August of 1962, started the second part of my "sea year", that is, I would be shipping out on a merchant ship with an engineering cadet for the sea time required to get our license as Third Mate or Third Engineer. That part would last until December, at which time we would return to the Academy to complete that year's academics. I checked with the Area Shipping Officer in New York and was told that I have been assigned to the American Presidents Line's, SS President Monroe. She was an older ship but she was unique in that she had five hatches for cargo and accommodations for 125 passengers. We would be leaving from Hoboken, New Jersey for a 4 month around the world voyage heading Westbound.

There is something very exhilarating about finally getting out on the ocean. I always like to walk the ship from stem to stern to get to know her. Standing up on the bow with the wind in your hair and looking down at the dolphins playing in the wake caused by the sharp bow cutting through the water offers a measure of freedom and excitement. This trip was going to be special because of our route. How many other 20 year olds get to do what I was embarking on that first day out, taking a trip around the world.

After departing New York Harbor, we made cargo stops in Philadelphia, Baltimore, Charleston and Savannah. Then it was off to the Panama Canal. I had been through once before in the prior year, but traversing one of the wonders of the world was still something unforgettable and couldn't be missed. I felt sorry for my cadet engineering partner, Charlie Polsen, because he was stuck down in the engine room and missed it all. In fact, he would miss most of the port arrivals and departures because he was always in the engine room when we were maneuvering. I, as deck cadet, was always on the bridge or on deck, forward or aft for tying up or letting go the mooring lines.

The Chief Mate set my work schedule and he was happy to get a cadet who knew the ropes from experience and not "green around the gills." At sea, I was to stand watch with 2nd Mate, the navigator, from 0400 to 0800, then work with the bosun on deck for 4 hours during the day. It was expected that I would be on the Bridge for evening "stars" and in fact I had my own sextant and took stars with the 2nd Mate for morning and night stars and the "noon" sunline. This was a time prior to GPS, so getting star fixes was not only fun but necessary. It required identifying a star in the sky, something you get pretty good at when you do it twice a day. In plebe year we signed up for the astronomy class because it was advertised as the course where you get to "study heavenly bodies", so we were already introduced to identifying stars and their constellations. You have to go out on the wing of the bridge and then get the angle that the star is at, relative to the horizon. It had to be accurate to the degrees, minutes and seconds at which time you start your stopwatch and run into the chart room to note the time on the ship's chronometer plus the angle you got with the sextant. You do this for several stars, at least four, and then begin the mathematical calculations to transfer that angle and time into a line of position on your chart. They never match up perfectly, but the small triangle generated is usually accurate to about 5 or 6 miles which is close enough on a 7.000 mile ocean voyage. Captains and Chief Mates know that when a Mate is constantly getting perfect fixes, he's cheating.

My on-deck duties working with the bosun were greasing cargo boom pulleys, splicing 3" lines to make cargo slings for unloading bales and any other general maintenance jobs needed to keep her shipshape and looking good. After leaving the Canal, we headed North up the Mexican coast. Our first passenger stop was to be Acapulco, a very beautiful Mexican port. The 2nd Mate was young, late 20s, and he had radioed ahead and chartered a ski boat for us to do some water skiing. When I was growing up, if a chance presented itself to go water skiing, I was there. We had a great time with the ski boat and even anchored her at a small beach, swam ashore and had a "cervasa" on beach chairs under an umbrella. The passengers boarded launches to take them on day trips into Acapulco. Perfect weather made it a glorious day.

We made cargo stops in Los Angeles and San Francisco which were also great places to visit for the passengers. Cargo stops were actually all great for the passengers because there were no containers then and loading and unloading could take several days. Practically all the passenger cabins were occupied.

I had a cousin who lived in Los Angeles and when I contacted him, he came to the pier and gave me a car to use for our stay. Charlie and I went to all the tourist attractions including Hollywood and Palas Verdi. It was my first time on the West Coast.

The deck officers aboard the Monroe included Captain "Bud" Kenny, the Chief Mate who was second in command and also oversaw all cargo operations and the watch standers, the 2nd

Mate and (2) 3rd Mates. The Captain's nickname was "Bud the stud", a tall handsome gent who had a special way with all the lady passengers. Additionally, he was a sober man, very competent and a friendly personality.

American President Lines had a very efficient cargo system. After each cargo watch, the mate in charge would enter each hatch and with a tape measure, calculate the empty cubic feet of cargo space. This would sent to the booking agents to try to fill the ship completely.

This ship also had a Steward's Department to cater to the 125 passengers. The Chief Steward was a Kings Pointer who had graduated with both his 3rd Mate and 3rd engineer's license. He sailed on each license and worked his way up to get both a Captain's and Chief Engineer's license. This trip was his last as Chief Steward since he was going to Law School when this trip was over. He had some background for Admiralty Law. This ship also carried a stewardess to oversee the room service and tending to the deck officer's rooms as well. Her name was Vina Hale, a middle aged woman who had been to sea her whole life. She was a lot of fun and was very knowledgeable about all the places to which we were going to travel.

After the West Coast, it was off to Honolulu, Hawaii for a 24 hour stop strictly for the passengers. My boss, the chief Mate had conferred with the Chief Engineer to let the engine cadet and myself off for the whole 24 hours. Charlie and I went up to the head of the pier and rented a pink and white striped open air jeep and two surf boards. We had a little money because we hadn't spent any of the $105.00/month we were paid as cadets. The first stop was Waikiki Beach to try surfing. That beach is unique in that there is a shallow water shelf that stretches ½ mile out sea where it then drops off to the depths. The waves crest out there and you can ride them all the way to shore, the whole ½ mile. We had the big boards, so it was easy to stand to ride the wave. We circumnavigated the entire Island of Oahu in our Jeep over the rest of the day, witnessing the gigantic waves being ridden by the pros on the North Shore. Some of the waves they riding were 35' high. We toured the Diamond Head volcano area and even went through a few pineapple farms. We stayed out the entire 24 hours sampling the night life on Waikiki Beach. We we were two tired cadets going back to our ship. My only regret, in hind sight, was not visiting the Pearl Harbor Memorial.

From Hawaii, it was a long ocean voyage to our next port of call, Yokohama, Japan. In addition to our shipboard duties, each cadet was given by the Academy, a "sea project" to complete. My deck cadet project covered topics that we could solve because we were directly aboard ship: stability, cargo stowage, ventilation, navigation and the like.

Unlike my last trip to the western Pacific, the weather was serene. We entered Yokohama harbor early in the morning and it was beautiful. There is a large U.S. Navy presence in the sister port of Yokosuka. We actually spent close to week there with much discharging of cargo and then reloading. I would stand cargo watches during the day and then would be free to go ashore and explore at night. It was a great time and the Japanese people were very friendly. I got my first taste of sushi in Yokohama when one of the stevedore bosses invited me to join him for dinner at an authentic Japanese restaurant. He told me I'd be the only "round eye" in the place. We had soup and then he offered me to try what he was having. I did and promptly ran into the men's room and heaved it all. So much for sushi, to this day.

Our Japanese journey included after Yokohama, to two short stays in Nagoya and Shimizu and then on to Kobe where we stayed for almost a week as well. While in Kobe my shipboard life would change dramatically when the junior 3rd Mate passed away. He was an elderly man who was making one last trip to complete 20 years at sea and would qualify him for a pension. It was very sad since he was a pleasant man and good shipmate. The Captain wired the home office in San Francisco asking for a replacement but was told no one could be found to fly out to Japan.

I was called up to the Captain's stateroom where he and the Chief Mate were waiting. I hadn't spoken to the Captain very much, but he told me that the Chief Mate felt I was ready to take over as junior 3rd Mate and would assume all of his duties. I was going to stand my own watch. Wow!! We went to the American Embassy where I was officially signed on as 3rd Officer.

For the balance of the port time in Kobe, I stood my cargo watch just like the 2nd and the other 3rd and now I was in charge. It's quite a different experience taking on that kind responsibility, even with the Chief Mate making himself available to me as needed. On cargo watch, I was the one now measuring the cubic feet in the holds.

Our next port of call was Chi Lung, Taiwan. When I came up to the bridge for my first "at-sea" watch, the Captain was right with me. He grilled me on what would or should I do in various situations meeting or overtaking other vessels. He was impressed that I could recite the Rules of the Road verbatim. He assured me if I had any doubts whatsoever, I was to call him using the phone directly to his room on the bridge. He was really very helpful in a friendly manner and I enjoyed his company. That didn't last though, because after two four hour watches, I didn't see him again. I guess he thought I was ready. Speaking of meeting other vessels at sea, I would love to, at night, utilize my morse code skills by using the signal light on each bridge wing. If I saw a ship approaching to pass us, I would signal "BT" : dash-dot-dot-

dot-dash, which was code for what ship? Most times there was a junior third Mate on the same watch over there and we would have a short conversation until we were too far away. I was the only officer who did that….the new kid!!

Going from $105.00 per month to $650.00 per month, plus overtime was really welcome. I made OT every day because the junior 3rd had to relieve the 2nd for dinner each evening. I would stand my noon to 4:00PM bridge watch and then at 5:00 I would return to the bridge while he ate giving me a half hour of OT every day. I would then go to bed only to be awakened for the midnight to 4:00AM watch. My new status moved me out of the Cadet's room and into the Mate's room. This also meant that as an officer, my room was kept up by the Stewardess. It was taboo for Cadets to mingle with the passengers, but now I was eating in the main lounge with them.

The Captain informed us that the family of the deceased Mate had notified the company that they would prefer him to have an at-sea burial. We had kept him in the freezer up to this point. The bosun was given a roll of canvas, waxed string, a palm and needle for sewing canvas, a number of old shackles for weight and a bottle of whiskey. He took it all back to the fantail along with the body and sewed him up for the burial. At 10:00AM on a Sunday morning, all the officers not on watch, assembled on the boat deck in dress white uniforms. The Captain already had two urns with people's ashes in them whose families also requested an at-sea burial so he figured he'd do all three at once. The 3rd Mates canvas bag was placed on a plywood platform and after a short prayer, the platform was raised and he slid into the sea. The first urn was uncapped and the contents poured out. The ship lurched, an odd gust of wind hit the boat deck and bits of ashes and bone sprayed all over our dress whites. Rumor had it that the second urn was flushed into the sea in the Captain's head. It was a bit disgusting.

It rained the whole time in Taiwan and standing cargo watches was very wet. There were large tents placed over each hold with a slit in one side to allow cargo in and out. If you had the watch you were to be out there on deck watching. My own foul weather gear was soaked through and through so one of the stevedore bosses gave me a set of the local foul weather gear. I wore a round pointed hat and a chest and back protector all made out of bamboo. I looked like a walking tiki hut. The Chief couldn't find me on deck and made an announcement: "will the junior 3rd mate please report to the Chief's office." When he saw me, he literally fell off his chair laughing and took my picture.

We departed Taiwan heading for Hong Kong across the South China Sea and one evening an encounter was made that caused me use that direct phone to the Captain's cabin. The night and the sea were black with no stars or moon to light them. There was nothing in front of my ship and then there was several hundred lights from fishing vessels illuminated across my bow. The Captain was quickly there and I asked, " should I put the engine room on standby?" He said "no Mr. Mate, they are just letting you know that they see you and for us not to change course. They will maneuver out of our way." I have to admit, I was scared at first and the Captain knew that and said I did right by calling him. Sure enough, they all moved clear like the Red Sea parting for Moses.

We arrived in Hong Kong just before sun-up and the city was still lit up. It vies for being one of the most beautiful harbors in the world. Hong Kong was also known then to be the best place to buy anything. Now having some money in my pocket, I bought things. Indian tailors came aboard selling custom made clothing and I got measured up. I wound up looking very sharp with my silk suit, cashmere overcoat and custom made shirts. Another man came aboard with a Florsheim shoe catalog. You pick out a style, he measures your feet and in two days you get the most comfortable pair of shoes ever worn. No break-in required. Electronics are another bargain and I bought all my Christmas presents right there in Hong Kong.

We were there for five days. I had done a midnight to 0800 cargo watch and collapsed into my bunk right after. At 0900, I jumped out of my bed thinking that the ship exploded. I put on pants and ran outside to see what happened. The company decided to repaint the deck house of the ship. Over 300 Chinese workers with hand held chipping hammers, all started at once when their supervisor blew his whistle. It was an unbelievable racket. They chipped the coatings right down to bare metal. This apparently was the first time this was done since she was built. You could see the paint layers showing her history, back to when she was all gray in World War II. They chipped the house bare in a couple of hours, applied rust proofing and a final coat in one day. Amazing!!

I did manage to ride on the near vertical tram to the top of Mt. Victoria The view of the harbor and Kowloon were spectacular and a large group of U.S. Navy's ships were anchored and enhanced it more.

After Hong Kong, it was off to Malaysia where Singapore was then it's capital. We stayed only a short time, staying at anchor and cargo delivered to us by barge. From there we went to Penang, also in Malaysia and also a very short stay.

Continuing westward we stopped in Ceylon (now Sri Lanka), known for getting really good deals on jewelry. I bought an opal brooch for my mother and a string of pearls for my Aunt Lucy. The first price quoted for the really beautiful brooch was $110.00. The stewardess was there with me and she took over the bargaining. I walked out with the pin costing me $10.00 US. The $250.00 string of pearls finally cost me $80.00. She was obviously well experienced here.

We had a number of crewmembers who loved to play softball and formed a team. I was on that team and played catcher. Our first game was against the American Embassy staff in Calcutta, India. The Embassy staff built their bench with cases of beer and they shared generously. It was a great time.

The poverty in India was everywhere with each street thick with beggars. Children were maimed to make them more sympathetic beggars. It was extremely depressing. The only nice places to go were the English clubs in certain sections of the city. There weren't even any of those at our next port of Cochin, India. We did get to play softball there, but the poverty was worse. Our whole team would bring food or vital items ashore with us to hand out to the people.

Because our ship had 125 passenger, a doctor was a required member of the crew. We were at Bombay and at anchor awaiting for a berth up in the harbor. There was a woman passenger aboard who was sick enough that our doctor said she required hospitalization.

Making contact via radio with the launch service to come out and pick her up was not working. The captain called for me to try the signal lamp that I had been practicing with at sea. I found out that all the mates has forgotten the morse code. I checked with the Coast Pilot, got the call sign of the service and contacted them. The launch was on the way.

We did eventually get a berth and we went into the port. When that woman rejoined the ship, she looked me up for a personal thank you.

In Bombay a new 3rd Mate was flown out and he joined the ship there. Thus ended my 3rd Officer status and I was very sad about it, having become very comfortable at that job. What other Academy, University or College would prepare a 20 year old to comfortably take over the responsibility of being in charge on a watch of eight hours per day over a multi-million dollar ship with a couple of hundred people aboard.

Still westward, we sailed into the harbor of Karachi, Pakistan. Back to being a cadet once again, I had more freedom in port. Charlie and I went to the what appeared to be the nicest building in all of Karachi, the Metropole Hotel. In the lobby, there was sign showing the activities of the day. There was to be a party in the main hall for all the various Ambassadors from embassies in Karachi and it was sponsored by the American Ambassador. Charlie and I decided to crash the party!

Dressed in our squeaky clean white formal uniforms, off we went. I remember some lady passengers out on deck whistling at us. When we entered the lobby, we were surprised to see US Marines at the entry to the Grand Ballroom. We thought, "Oh well, that's it." We walked up to beg to get in when they both came to attention, saluted and said "Good evening, Sirs." We were in.

I spotted a table occupied by younger people who invited us to sit. I sat next to a beautiful girl who had the cutest Swedish accent to her English. She was the daughter of the Swedish Ambassador. We danced away that night, exchanging stories of our backgrounds.

I really liked her and asked if we could correspond and keep in touch. She said she didn't think her father would approve. When asked why she said: "because I'm 13 years old. She sure looked older.

It was a fun night anyway and who would expect that in Karachi.

I had made two passages of the Panama Canal and we were now to transit Suez Canal from the Red Sea to the Mediterranean

Sea. There are no locks in the Suez and nothing like the jungles of Panama. The north shore of the canal is pure desert, sand as far as you can see.

The south side is manicured agricultural land growing crops. We had a Russian Pilot take us through. He said he always asked to do the American ships because the food was better.

Our first stop after the Suez Canal was Alexandria, Egypt. The passengers were taken to view the Pyramids, but the trip was too long for those of us working on the ship. The big tourist item to buy in Egypt was camel saddles. You could get the plain ones for $15.00, on up to the super fancy engraved leather cushions with brass caps for $50.00. I would guess that between the passengers and the crew, there were 300 camel saddles on the Monroe. The saddles made great ottoman's and conversation pieces.

After a short stop in Tunis, we did a big circle in the Mediterranean, starting with Barcelona, Spain. There were no bullfights to see on the day we were there, but the city was beautiful and the food was fabulous. We let the waiter order for us and what a treat it was. For a twenty year old, I was becoming quite the connoisseur.

Next was Marseilles, France. A beautiful young girl, who I was guessing to be about my age, came aboard to sell French perfumes to the passengers. She spoke English and I stayed with most of the time she was aboard. We were staying over night there, so I asked her out to dinner. When she finished selling, she had to call her father to ask permission to join me. Very sadly, he said his daughter was not going out with an American. I thought to myself, if it wasn't for America, that father would be speaking German today, if at all.

If I was ever going to take a trip later in life to Europe, the one place high on my list is Italy. We arrived in Genova and the longshoremen in all of Italy went out on strike. We had cargo for and we were scheduled to pick up cargo in Genova, Livourno and Napoli, so we were stuck there. I don't think I heard anyone complain. I went to the USO for entertainment at night and met one of the local hostesses who volunteer at the Club. She invited me to join her and her girlfriend for a day at the beach in San Remo, the Italian Riviera. You can imagine this Catholic boy from Brooklyn, when the girls took off their tops. A jump into the cool Sea helped.

I took a train from Genova to Milano. Figuring which train to get on is impossible: Directo, directisimo, rapido, rapidisimo. I got on one that sounded like it was the fastest only to be on one that stopped at every stop. It was pleasant though with locals selling bread and wine at various stops. It was all home made and very good. I remember that a bottle of Ruffino Chiante in the basket cost $.33. Milano is a gorgeous city especially around the cathedral. The "saint" statues on multiple spires around the roof of the church are made stretching them very tall, so from the ground they look normal. The people of Milano are mostly blond haired and blue eyed with light skin. Of course, when in that city, you had to see the famous opera house, La Scala and it was worth the trip.

Our stay in Livourno was a short one and I never even got ashore.

Napoli was a different story, since we stayed there for almost a week. I took a train to Roma from there and it is a place everyone should see. I had a book, "Europe on $5.00 per day" (1962). After visiting the Vatican and St. Peter's Basilica, I followed directions in the book to a place to eat. I walked two blocks and up a set of wooden stairs and knocked on the door. It was a woman's house with three tables in the living room. She welcomed me in and sat me at a table. She poured me a glass of her home made wine from a Pepsie bottle. It was delicious, as was the pasta, sauce and bread. The whole dinner cost me $1.25 and I was full. Rome is so spectacular where we at home think things are old when they are 300 years old. There are things in Rome that are 5000 years old. Back in Napoli, you had to go see the San Francisco Bar, home of the deported gangster, Lucky Luciano. And he was there. By the end of the 3 weeks in Italy, I was starting to get by speaking limited Italian.

It was a great country to visit at the close of this circumnavigation of the globe because we headed back to New York harbor when we sailed. I'll never forget that when we were entering New York under the under-construction Veranzano Bridge, the store keeper was on the bow with me. He said, "You know cadet, wherever I go around this world, I thank the Lord, that I was born in the good old USA." I had to agree.

Just an aside, I still could identify, by company, most of the tugboats plying the waters of New York Harbor.

United States Lines S.S. President Monroe

CHAPTER 13
Summer Adventure 1963

After stowing Gretel away in 1962 at the KP waterfront, Graham Hall, Bob Lindmark and myself had to go home to pack up and report in to the Area Shipping Officer for our second half of our sea year.

When we returned to Academy after the Christmas holiday, we went right back into the school and classes and studying mode. Graham and I were once again room mates. One day shortly after classes started, we got a notice to report to Admiral McLintock's office, the Superintendent of the Academy. Oh Boy!!! What did we do?

After waiting a good period in his outer office, conjuring up thoughts of what was about to come down, we were told to enter. He looked up from his desk and a big smile came across his face, stood up , shook our hands and told us to sit. He proceeded to tell us of a great letter he received from one Cornelius Sheilds of the NY Stock Exchange, explaining how he met three fine young men up at Newport, RI who were Cadets at his Academy. He said that we were great representatives of Kings Point and how impressed he was with what we did with our Monomoy and where we had traveled. He added to his letter a check for $350.00 to be given to us to make the changes we described to him and to fix her up for the next voyage. The one condition he set was that we would stop by Larchmont Yacht Club on our way East to give him a day sail. Of course, Admiral McLintock had no clue of what we had done the previous year, so we had to explain it all in detail. We were there for an hour. We guessed that he told his wife, Winnie, all about our adventure because she contacted us insisting that she would get to crash the champagne bottle across the bow when we relaunched her.

We had another very busy Sailing Team season, but whenever we had any free time it was spent fixing up our boat. The dock crew flipped her over giving us access to redo the caulking that we didn't do a very good job of last year. She leaked like crazy. After we redid that job, they flipped her right side up and Bob got going on his project for her. He installed a bow sprit, so we could make her cutter rigged with two jibs. What a job he did! We also made the minor improvements we wanted but couldn't afford before. We changed her name from Gretel, since Wetherly trounced the Australian challenger the previous Fall in just 5 races. The day came in July that we were going to launch "Venture Galley" named after Blackbeard the pirate's vessel. The Admiral's wife came down, to crash the champagne bottle and the first time she tried, the bottle didn't break. The second time it did break but the champagne inside was well shaken, so the bottle exploded. A shard of glass hit Bob in the neck knicking his carotid artery, so we had to rush him to the hospital to stop the bleeding and get sewn up. We hoped this was not an omen.

The next day we stepped her mast and towed her around to our mooring in Kings Point park. Our caulking job worked really well this time and she stayed dry while on the mooring, except if it rained.

Once again, the day arrived that we would begin our second adventure and head Down East. Our first stop was at Larchmont Yacht Club, to fulfill our promise to take Mr. Sheilds for a day sail and show him the improvements we made. He liked it and told us if ever get into any trouble please give him a call.

On the second day, when we were abeam of Bridgeport, CT and moving along quickly on a broad reach with the wind out of the South. We were sitting on the gunnel on the high side. None of us looked behind us to see a strong gust kicking up white caps and heading right at us. When the realization hit us we all dove for the cleated down main and jib sheets to loosen the sails. In a matter of seconds, Venture Galley turned turtle, that is she was flipped completely over. We all jumped overboard and then climbed back onto the hull. To my surprise, up popped my waterproof duffle bag with all my gear in it. The others were not so lucky. We actually were laughing at the fate of our adventure. In hindsight, I think the three of us were so comfortable on the water that none of us were afraid because of what happened.

We did not know that Bridgeport was the home of Sikorsky Helicopters who would test fly their new helicopters out over Long Island Sound. As such, they kept a rescue boat near Bridgeport Harbor and somebody there spotted our flipped over boat and dispatched their boat. When they got to us, they were perplexed as to what to tie on to, in order to tow us in. I had them throw the tow line to us. I dove off our boat, took the line and dove under water and tied it to the steel bracket that Bob installed to hold down the bow sprit. They began the tow with the boat flipped, sails fluttering underwater and three giddy guys on top. They brought us to the Black Rock Yacht club where the Club members could not have been more helpful. They helped us right the boat and then put 5 or 6 electric bilge pumps into the flooded hull. She was bone dry in about 2 hours. We were also allowed to stay at the Yacht Club until we were ready to go. Now Bob and Graham had nothing, no extra clothes, no wallets and no money. As such, Graham went to the telephone and explained to our benefactor, Mt. Sheilds, our current fate. He instructed him to go to the Western Union store up the street and there would be cash awaiting for them. From there, they went to a discount sporting goods store and got clothes, sleeping bags and then some food. Fortunately, nothing on boat was damaged, so once we were restocked, we resumed our voyage and headed for Mystic Seaport, the whaling museum in Mystic, CT.

We had heard the Seaport Museum curator was a Kings Pointer. That turned out not to be true, but the currant Curator let us stay there anyway. Bob and Graham went exploring and I stayed back to bail out the boat. The wonderful job we did on the caulking got blown out because of the capsizing, so we were back to bailing. A very snobby lady from a neighboring yacht came by and looked down at me working and said "my, my, what clean bilge water you have." I said "it should be lady, we change it three times a day." The next day, it was off to Narragansett Bay. The weather for sailing was absolutely perfect so we were thoroughly enjoying ourselves.

I had contacted my cousin Ernest McVay who lived in Riverside, RI and was Commodore of the Barrington Yacht Club. Ernest was actually Dr. McVay, an Ophthalmological Surgeon, specializing in children's crossed eyes, plus he's an avid sailor. He also loved racing and took part in most Block Island Race Weeks and the Bermuda Races. He was the same cousin whose boat my Dad borrowed for that family trip to Block Island. He invited us to his home and arranged a berth for us. We went to dinner and he asked if we would like join him and my Aunt Evelyn aboard his Block Island 40, now Tango 4, for a weekend sail to Block Island. Yes! Yes!! It was a beautiful boat with perfect weather for the weekend. We picked up a mooring in the Old Harbor of Block Island and went ashore to do a little exploring. My Mom had told me that she lived one summer on Block Island before I was born. My Dad was Mate and my Grandfather, George McVay was the Captain of the New London/Block Island ferry named the "Pemaquid." It was a fabulous weekend for which we were most grateful. We stayed a couple of days extra because Graham met a beautiful girl named Didi and he wanted to see where that would go. Didi's father took us out on his stinkpot...err, sorry, a beautiful 36' powerboat. The Rhode Island coastal area was very beautiful. When we were leaving, Didi baked us a cake made to look like our boat. Nice girl.

It was such a letdown to go from that beautiful yacht back to our own vessel. We left the Yacht Club heading South and got becalmed in Narragansett Bay and had to spend the night in a small cove on Prudence Island. The next day, the wind blew strong making it an easy sail to Woods Hole Oceanographic Institute located on the Southwest corner of Cape Cod. Unfortunately, the strong wind and three sails caused a compression fracture at the top of the mast. The kind folks at the Institute had their boat repair people work with Bob to make a repair to completely cure the problem. We toured the impressive campus and they let us stay the night at one of their docks. Boating people are so nice and helpful to other boaters.

Our next stop was Hyannis Port harbor on the south coast of Cape Cod, Massachusetts. While ashore there, we met four nice girls. Hyannis Port has a breakwater surrounding the port much like Point Judith's Harbor of Refuge, making it inviting to go out to the outer section for me to do some spearfishing on the following day. We invited the girls to join us and they accepted. After the short trip out, we dropped the anchor and over I went. In a matter of a half hour, we had four eight or nine pound Tautaug. Out of seemingly nowhere, there was a helicopter hovering over us with a loud speaker ordering us to head to shore immediately. We asked our passengers: "does anybody know what is going on", when one of the girls said "maybe I should have told you and my dad where I was going, since my Dad is the Chief of Police for Hyannis Port." When we tied up at public dock, there were several police men including the Chief waiting for us. When explanations were given, the Chief actually invited us to his home. Spotting the fish, he said "bring them along and that'll be supper." The girl's grandfather was a sailing enthusiast, especially the old square riggers, priding himself on being able to name each sail on those ships. Graham was our resident expert on that subject and got along famously with Grandpa. We had a great evening and left happy and full to sleep aboard Venture Galley.

We agreed that it was about time to head West and home to Kings Point. The chances of our finding another tug and barge to tow us home were slim to none. Our luck did not leave us yet because when we passed through The Race between Fishers Island and Orient Point, LI with a fair incoming tide, a northeaster storm developed giving us fair winds. We spent the next three days in foul weather gear because of the rain, but the wind blew us back down the Sound. It was a happy ending to our final voyage on the Venture Galley.

Upon arrival at Kings Point, the dock crew told us that they had a visit from a representative of the Marblehead Massachusetts Sailing School. He was looking for a sailing Monomoy for his school. Our dock crew told him of us and asked them to give him a call upon our return. Graham gave him a call and after a 20 minute discussion, we all agreed to sell the Venture Galley to them for $500.00. Two days later a truck came to pick her up and she was gone. We were a little sad to see her go, but we were a little richer and full of rich memories.

Second Class year started right away, so it was back to living on campus.

The Venture Galley as a cutter rigged, sloop with one mainsail and two jibs. Lindmark's bow sprit was necessary.

CHAPTER 14

Coming off the great summer of 1963, we came back to the full academic pressure of studying to finish our degree requirements and prepare for our License Week of testing. On top of that Graham and I were elected Co-Captains of the Sailing Team. On top of that, I was appointed a Cadet Officer on the 2nd Battalion Staff. It was too much and I didn't have time to do any one job correctly and keep up with my academics. For the first time, my 1st quarter QPA dropped to 1.91 out of 4.0. The Academy's Dean, Captain Sanford Lamouse, told me in no uncertain terms that I had to do whatever was necessary to get my grades up. The Sailing Team's second quarter schedule was minimal. I resigned as a member of the Battalion Staff and I had to move out of my room on Battalion Staff Row. My plan to improve the most important thing at this point, my grades, was to ask for help and when agreed to, I moved in with my classmate, Gene Owens. Gene was a great guy and happened to have a QPA over the past 3 years of over 3.50 out of 4.00, a Gold Star student and obviously had good study habits. And isn't that just what I needed? I limited my Sailing Team activity to weekends and concentrated all extra time to studying. It worked! My second quarter grades qualified me to wear a Silver Star, coming in at 3.1. That got the Dean off my case and brought my two quarter average up to a safe level. Thank you Gene.

I am having a difficult time describing what took place in October of 1963. Paul, Marion and their infant Paul, my God child, were in their new Volkswagen "bug" just sitting waiting at a light when a driver of a Corvette lost control of his car and slammed into them. Paul was really injured badly and Marion's pelvis was broken in 8 places. The windshield popped out and the infant was tossed out through the hole onto a lawn suffering a broken arm. Getting this news about two of my closest friends was devastating. This happened in Norwalk, CT where they lived. I could not leave the Academy to go see either of them, so I had to rely on phone calls home to get the latest news. It made me think about best friends. You may not see each other for what is sometimes long periods. When you do finally get together, you pick up right where you left off, as though you were never too far apart. I was hoping that we could get back to that realization. It wasn't going to happen. The baby Paul's injuries were all fixable and he was going to be fine. Marion's injuries were going to require months of recuperation and healing. Paul had many internal injuries that left his condition very serious. After a few days, it was determined that Paul had to have his spleen removed, a very important organ that fights bacteria, viruses and infections.

That was a worrisome move for everyone. There was a good cause for worry because the worst thing happened. Paul contracted pneumonia and passed away. I could not imagine the grief felt by Marion and also Paul's Dad, Matt Daniti, losing his only son and my grief as well. I managed to get a special pass to go to the funeral home that night and the Mass early the next morning.

McLaughlen's Funeral parlor was absolutely jammed with people who all knew each other from the neighborhood. I remember coming to the door of the packed room where Paul was laid out and everyone there turned and looked at me, whispering out loud "there's his best friend." I lost it; I could not enter the room and wound up going to the downstairs lounge and wept loudly. I could not go in to see my best friend from when we were 4 and 5 years old, one with whom I did so much and one who was so much a part of my life. My memory of the rest of the night is blurred. I attended the funeral the next day, after which, I had to return to Kings Point. Fortunately, I was able to call to Marion's parents house to get updates on her condition. Marion told me later that her father really stepped up for her, moving into their apartment, so he could be with her during her recuperation, every day. When Paul Jr. was sufficiently healed, Marion's dad brought him to he and his wife Mae's home in Brooklyn. I kept tabs on them and Marion went home to her parents home after six weeks in the hospital.

During our 1st Class year, one thing related to our summer adventures of sailing around the Northeast, was the contact made with Cornelius Shields. Mr. Shields belonged to Larchmont Yacht Club which hosted Larchmont Race week, where the crews of many classes of one design sailboats would test there skills at racing. It was a very prestigious event but Mr. Shields thought they needed a new design to help modernize the fleet. He designed a 30' sloop to accomplish that mission. His first order was for 15 boats of the new Shields Class and the first five were donated to Kings Point. When he came to the Academy to make the presentation, Graham and I were asked to be with Admiral McClintock during noon lunch with the Regiment, where he presented a plaque with a half model of the boat. That plaque was later used as the trophy for Shields class events.

The second five boats went to NY State Maritime College across the Sound and the third five went to the US Naval Academy. That gave us a local fleet of ten boats close aboard. The ten boat fleet made its debut at Larchmont race week that year. We had a shortage of crew from the Sailing Team that weekend. I could only get one under classman for my boat, so I invited my brother Don to join me. Race Week was sailed out in the middle of Long Island Sound with the windward mark set to the West because of the Westerly breeze. The Sheilds Class was privileged enough to be allowed to debut the new class and go off first of that huge fleet. We accomplished the first three legs of the race with all 10 boats fairly close to each other. When we rounded the leeward mark, nine boats of the fleet came close hauled on the starboard tack and headed out to the center of the Sound. I remembered from our summer adventures on our Monomoy, that the ebb current running at that time, ran very strong out in the middle, so I took my boat to a series of short tacks along the coast, out of the current. Once I determined that I could make the finish line on one starboard tack, off we went. The three of us, including my thrilled brother, won the very first Shields Class race.

The sailing team was very strong for that year with a lot of talented 1st classmen along with a good crop of under classmen as well. Graham Hall was the strongest sailor amongst us, with Bob Lindmark, myself, good sailors like Bob McEliece and the younger sailors with whom we were winning regattas in our Middle Atlantic Division quite handily. I remember we had a plebe, a good sailor, Stan Smith from Saudie Daisie, Tennessee. I recall asking him "what is Saudie Daisie, TN and he replied ...Golly, it's a big town and we've got over 4,000 people there." I told him I'm from Brooklyn, NY and we've got 5,000 people in my apartment house. He was a great kid and competitor. Our MAISA win record (Middle Atlantic Intercollegiate Sailing Association) qualified us to attend the Nationals for the 3rd year with this one out in Newport Beach, CA. We came in third in the Nation with Graham being named "Intercollegiate Sailor of the Year."

As 1st Classmen and as Team Captains of a Varsity sport, Graham and I were invited to a meeting of the Block M Club. The Block letter M stood for Mariners and was awarded to those sports participants who lettered in a varsity sport. The purpose of the meeting was to plan the annual Block M party which consisted of renting a hall, ordering music, supplying refreshments and most importantly getting female college students to attend. It was the closest thing to a Frat party that was possible in a Federal Academy. Graham and I really got into it and sent invitations to mostly girl's colleges, but others as well, all within a 25 mile radius of Kings Point. Cadets who earned a Varsity Letter were invited. We wound up renting the Knights of Columbus Hall in Great Neck, the big town next to Kings Point, and while there doing the rental paperwork, I met the Rheingold beer salesman. Sean O'Rourke, the salesman, was my classmate for 8 years in St. Patrick's elementary school in Bay Ridge. How lucky was that and we got a very good deal on refreshments. The party was a roaring success and our invitation scheme brought more girls to the party than there were Cadets. It was there that I met a girl who I really liked.

June was a local Long Island girl who was not in college but came with a girl friend who heard of our party. She was a beautician, which was obvious with her perfect hair enhancing her already good looks. And she was a fantastic dancer. We hit it off from the outset and her working on Saturdays meshed perfectly with my sailing team obligations for a date on the following Saturday night…..and on the next one after that…and after that. I hit it off with her parents as well and it wasn't long before I would spend those Saturday nights at her house. I also brought her to Brooklyn to meet my Mom and Aunt Lucy. June and I were actually dating like we were ready to go to the next level and in fact we got engaged shortly after graduation. I am ahead of myself here and I'll come back to this later.

Life in that Fall of 1963 had another ugly and sad twist to it as well. I remember sitting in anthropology class on that fateful day of November 22, 1963, when there was a knock on the door with our instructor being called out to the hall. When he came back he looked like he was going to faint and calmly told us that President Kennedy had been shot. We were all ordered to return to our barracks and await further instructions. I believe all military installations were put on alert for a short period. We all remembered that we marched in his inauguration parade, adding to the sorrow felt by us all.

CHAPTER 15

Our 1st Class year (January to June) became more intense as the pressure was building, not only to complete the academic requirements for our degrees, but more so for the preparation for the one solid week of tests known as License Week. NO ONE FLUNKS ANY PART OF LICENSE WEEK AT KINGS POINT!!! The Coast Guard monitored those five days while we were tested in all subjects required to get a Third Mate, Oceans, Any Gross Tons License for the Deckies or Third Assistant Engineer, Steam or Diesel, Any Horsepower for the Engineers.

Our tests (Mates) consisted of all those subjects that would make you a competent 3rd Officer aboard any ship regardless of her size or trade. Those would include the many facets of Navigation: Celestial, charts, LORAN-C, Radar Plotting problems and tides and currents. Also, there was Rules of the Road, signal lamp communications, stability, safety and ship procedures among others.

Having already served as 3rd Officer on the President Monroe for three months, some of the testing was a bit anti-climactic. I did not have problems with any part of the test week nor did anyone else. The Academy Administration was very happy with that result.

When I think back of going to this Federal Academy, how fortunate I was to have these four years. It had its excitement all the way through: the excitement and the pride to wear these sharp uniforms, having been selected to attend one of the nation's premier educational institutions, being ship wrecked, summer sailing adventures, being promoted to 3rd Mate while still a cadet, traveling around he world, sailboat competitions at a National Championship level and team co-captain.

All during my 1st Class year, my girlfriend, June and I had many wonderful times and I really felt that I loved her. It turned out that it was not a relationship that turned into a lifetime commitment. That causes me to not dwell on that subject any further here.

CHAPTER 16

Graduation

It was a beautiful day, weather wise and my whole family came to Kings Point for the ceremony, Mom, Aunt Lucy, Don, Edith and June. We all looked sharp in our dress white uniforms as we prepared to march on to Tomb Field. This was pretty new to me, since I hadn't marched in many parades because the Sailing Team always had regattas on the weekends. They freshly mowed the grass, so when we marched on, it kicked up all the pollen and dust aggravating my slight case of hay fever. As we paraded past the reviewing stand, I sneezed on every step as we were going by, thirteen straight sneezes in a row. After several speeches, the thrill that it was all over was culminated with the traditional hat toss and cheers. Oh what a past four years this experience has been. Afterwards, my family went to Peter Lugar's Steakhouse to celebrate.

There was no down time since my application to the American Officer's Organization (AMO) was approved and I had a job to go to 3 days after graduation. I was to join the SS Flying Fish, an American Export Isbrandsten ship, ready to leave on a four month, round the world voyage going Eastbound. We left from their terminal in Hoboken, NJ and I was the new Jr. Third Mate on this smaller, five hatch cargo ship. The Captain, Sven Colding, an old Dutchman, was originally with Isbrandtsen Lines before they were merged with American Export Lines. He was an eccentric man in his tee shirt and flip flops, who referred to his deck officers as "my young men." If fact, we were young, with most of the ship's officers being under 30 years of age. As Junior third, my watch at sea was 1200 to 1600 and then again midnight to 0400. I also relieved the 2nd Mate, Tom Sullivan, for dinner each evening for one half hour for him to eat. Tom and I became fast friends. He was a 1962 graduate of New York State Maritime College at Fort Schuyler in the Bronx. We departed Hoboken with our intended first port of call being Barcelona, Spain. It was an uneventful Atlantic Ocean crossing where we spent some time becoming totally familiar with the amounts, locations and destinations of all the cargo aboard. One thing that was not good with our Captain, was the fact that we were not allowed to use the Radar, only he could. It was an ancient thing with a 10" screen that looked like it was purchased at a yard sale and I think he was afraid of us blowing it up. He smoked these small cigars and he would smoke them leaving a long ash. The ash was left on the cone that was there to view the screen without glare. If that ash was disturbed, he knew that one of us tried to use the Radar and all hell broke loose. Fortunately, there was no fog crossing the Atlantic.

There was one terribly frightening incident for me that happened when we were transiting the Straits of Gibraltar. It was on the midnight to four watch when I saw in the distance, an approaching ship who's fore and aft running lights were aligned straight at us. As it got closer, with lights still aligned at us, I could make out that it was a passenger ship, well lit up. I determined that I would come to starboard, preparing for the standard port to port meeting. "If you are going to make a move, make it a bold one, so the other ship has no doubt of your intentions." A rule that was drilled into us. So, I changed course 15 degrees to starboard. When I accomplished that move, the other ship came to port the same amount, increasing the chance of a collision. I came to starboard more and she came to port more. I thought if I continued to starboard doing a 360 degree circle and he did the same, that we would collide anyway. So….I did what we are not supposed to do, I felt I was in extremis…."hard to port." As we passed close by, 2 to 3 hundred yards from her stern, the parties were in full swing over there with no one apparently aware of how close a call it was. Normal procedure on a merchant ship in open waters was try not to get closer than one mile apart. I thought: the ink isn't even dry on my license and I came close to losing it. I also learned that Captain Sven was not a light sleeper. Thank heavens!

It turned out that this younger crew of officers became quite friendly and we enjoyed each others company. We decided that, whoever was available, and when we were in a new country, we would go ashore together to enjoy the local cuisine and that we would go to an upscale restaurant to sample that food. I'll never forget the first excursion of our group in Barcelona. There were six of us there and while enjoying a glass of their best wine, we asked the Maitre 'd……….. "sir, please order for us!" It was superb, with giant Mediterranean prawns, a whole local fish deboned table side, and on and on. We had many memorable meals that became more exotic the further East we traveled.

From Spain, we went to Marseille, France, then two ports in Italy, Genoa and Naples.

As I had learned on the President Monroe as 3rd Mate, Port time meant working 8 hours per day on cargo watch. As junior 3rd Mate that also meant that my watch was the midnight to

8:00AM watch. If there was no cargo working in those hours, you still were the Officer in charge of the ship for that time period. Often it meant "welcoming" aboard our crew members who were out enjoying the local pleasures. During the course of the voyage, the deck officers came up with a scheme that allowed lengthy shore time for us. It consisted of three 8 hours on and 8 hours off watch standings, followed by one 32 hours off. Because we were a break bulk cargo ship, we often spent more than a few days in port, so it worked.

Operationally, the Eastern Mediterranean went smoothly, as did our passage through the Suez Canal. We stopped in Addis Ababa in Ethiopia. Talk about HOT! I had no money when we shipped out of New York harbor and I had bought a cheap pair of work boots, that had plastic soles and heels. I found myself stuck to the deck as my boots melted in the 123 degree heat. I had to borrow a pair until I could buy a decent pair. We did the standard ports in the Asian sub-continent: Karachi, Pakistan, three ports in India, Bombay, Cochin, Calcutta, the island nation of Ceylon and Singapore. We had quite a few thousand tons of cargo for the heating up area around Saigon in Vietnam which had been a war torn nation for a long time. The French were the first involved there and now we Americans were getting involved to try to stem the tide of Communism taking over Southeast Asia. We had to anchor out in the middle of the Saigon River for a week, waiting to get to the dock to unload. It did not take long to realize that we were in a war zone. There were nothing but rice paddies to the starboard. At night, you would hear and see helicopters dropping flares in the paddies followed by the chatter of machine gun fire. It was far enough away that we were not ducking incoming, but it was eerie enough just the same. One day we spotted MIG jets shooting rockets at the Presidential palace off in the distance. We had to stand our watches out on the deck. Thieves and prostitutes would paddle around ships in little canoes with grappling hooks and rope to get aboard unwatched decks. They would steal anything not firmly secured, including brass sounding tube covers. There was a market for brass. One of our engineers was horny enough that he lowered a line to a prostitute in a canoe. She climbed the line to his room and went in through the porthole. She went out the porthole as well after she drugged him and took all his valuables. We could not wait to get out of there.

The Flying Fish proceeded East to Hong Kong, then North to Taiwan and then Japan, where we would spend three weeks in four ports.

My sister Edith was getting married while I was away, so I assumed that I was going to miss the wedding. As our circumnavigation progressed, I began to see that her wedding date might coincide with the arrival of the Flying Fish on the West Coast port of San Francisco, where our port stay would be five to seven days. I made a deal with the other Mates that I would stand as many of their watches while in Japan, if they would cover for me in San Francisco. This was all contingent on the dates working, so I could fly from California to New York and back without missing the ship. Of course, I cleared it with the Captain who surprisingly agreed.

One thing I did do on the limited time I got ashore was buy a motorcycle at the newly opened Honda motors showroom. They had a few cars and an assortment of motorcycles. I bought one and drove it down to the ship where I got one of the longshore groups to lift it up on deck and I stowed it in one of the deck houses. She was a beauty with 55 CC's and nice looks all for $156.00.

The voyage from Yokohama, Japan to San Francisco took twelve days on a Great Circle route that took us way North of Hawaii. The daytime watch at sea for me was Noon to 1600 and was kind of boring as it was basically being a lookout from the bridge watching for traffic. There was nothing to see but ocean. Yet, about three days out, we were startled to put it lightly. A Russian submarine surfaced about 200 yards to starboard. There was a loud whoosh and Russian crew members came out on the top of the Sail. I think they were just as startled to see us so close, because they submerged as quickly as they came up.

There was no boredom on the night watches. The activities in the heavens at night were spectacular. Heading East at midnight, put you right at the front of the planet Earth traveling through the Universe. The shooting stars were plentiful and the occasional meteor lit up the night sky. There was one meteor that descended from above due South of us where Hawaii was located. It was so big and bright that I thought its presence would be reported by the news stations in our daily news briefs that our radio operator received. It went unmentioned.

SS *Flying Fish*

Our arrival back in the United States was a most unusual approach to the Port of San Francisco. The weather was overcast with a low cloud cover and misting rain. It created a lens type optical illusion that showed us the San Francisco skyline flipped upside down. The whole crew was up to see it. That city has a beautiful skyline plus the Golden Gate Bridge, upside down or not. As we got closer everything returned to normal. Our cargo requirements were going to keep us there for 5 or 6 days at least which included the weekend of my sister's wedding. So, after clearing it with my fellow officers, I was off to San Francisco International Airport. It was a 6 hour flight that cost $300.00 for the round trip. I picked up June after arriving at Idewild Airport and then went to Brooklyn where my Mom was hosting a dinner for the wedding party and relatives on the night before the wedding. As I walked in the door, my Mom was walking to the living

room with a tray of drinks that went flying when she spotted me. Edith was so happy to see me there and that made the effort to get there well worth it. I could even participate as an usher since I had my dress blues uniform at home. June was in the wedding party and it was wonderful seeing our neighborhood friends. Edith's husband, Joe Dropp, was committed to NOAA as an officer. Joe graduated from SUNY Maritime at Fort Schuyler, NY. It seemed like the weekend went by in an instant and I found myself back on the ship. June was not happy that I was gone again.

The rest of the trip went by quickly for me. We spent five days in Los Angeles, then headed South to transit the Panama Canal and for my first time going from the Pacific into the Atlantic. There were no stops on the East Coast until we entered New York harbor. When we were docking at Hoboken, NJ there was something special going on.

Chesterfield cigarettes was to film a commercial while docking the ship. "Here's Brian McAllister, Docking Pilot, directing the Tug Brian McAllister, docking The SS Flying Fish at Hoboken, NJ. Brian is a Chesterfield man." With that he lit up one of their cigarettes. "Come ahead on the Brian, he ordered the tug," and then he'd take a puff and look satisfied. "Cut and that is a take." I was the 3rd mate in the pilot house so I got to see the whole thing. It was the first time I would meet Brian McAllister. By the way, he threw the Chesterfield overboard and promptly lit up a Marlboro.

Captain Colding told me that on the following trip on the Fish, he wanted me to re-varnish the wood rails on the bridge wing. I told him that I would not be on the next trip and instead I would be working on tugboats like the Brian McAllister. He was mad "Vie would you vant to work on a little piece of shit like that." I just told him it was in my family blood.

Before arriving back in New York, I wondered how I was going to get my motorcycle home without a registration and license plate. My watch partner engineer actually made me a license plate that had Japanese language symbols on it. I was going to fake it. I only got as far as the Holland Tunnel when I was pulled over by the NYPD. "What the hell kind of plate is that?" was the first thing he said. I said, "Officer, that's a Japanese plate," and I handed him the bill of sale, all written in Japanese. "This is the registration." I pleaded that my understanding is, that a person making a foreign or out of state purchase was allowed 30 days to get the paperwork correct. I told him I just got off a ship that sailed around the world and that I bought the motorcycle in Yokohama. "Get the hell out of here and get it done."

I had several weeks off after that trip, during which time June and I were engaged despite her dissatisfaction with the long periods of my absence. I had to keep sailing on my license in order to qualify to get my Commission in the US Naval Reserve.

Getting a job on tugs was not as simple as hoped, so I answered a request by American Export Lines to join the SS Export Aide for an express trip to the Mediterranean. It was the Aides second voyage and we were to visit Cadiz and Barcelona, Spain, Marseilles, France and Genoa and Naples in Italy, all accomplished in six weeks. On our return to America, our first port of call was Providence, RI in the Northern end of Narragansett Bay. To get there required picking up a Pilot at the Bay entrance near Newport, RI. To my utter surprise, the elder gentleman who came aboard was the founder of the Narragansett Bay Pilot's Assn., Captain Howard McVay, my Grand Uncle. It was a reminder that the strongest presence of the McVay Clan was in the Providence, RI area.

My first attempt to apply for a tug job was with Moran Towing Corp. I figured that if their sales pitch was advertising themselves as "The Best in the Business," well then that is where I would want to be. I also remember my Dad saying "Moran is the best" but they go all over. Since I had been all over already, that did not bother me. Because I had little or no tugboat experience, I had to sail as an Able Seaman or deckhand first. "You can't be yelling orders from the pilothouse to the deckhands unless you have been on deck yourself." That is what I was told and I agreed. I will never forget my first job for Moran. I was told to report to Moran's yard in Port Richmond, Staten Island and board the Esther Moran. I rode over there from Brooklyn on my motorcycle. The Esther was Moran's biggest tug at the time. She was 127' LOA, 3600HP and she was equipped with a towing machine with a wire hawser instead of nylon rope. She was an inspected tug requiring me to sign on as an AB. We spent a couple of hours loading supplies and off we went for a trip up the Hudson River to Revena, NY to pick up the barge Adelaide, a 16,000 ton cement barge. The ebb current in the Hudson River was especially strong that morning and Moran tugs and docking pilot were attempting to get the HMS Queen Elizabeth into pier 92 on the West side of Manhattan. The current was making the docking more difficult, so when the pilot found out that the Esther was in the area, he requested our assistance. We came in on the stern of the Queen and lifted her safely into the dock. I can't forget that experience: "My first job working for Moran was docking the HMS Queen Elizabeth."

At Revena, NY, the barge was loaded and waiting for us. She had a small notch in the stern for the Esther to get into the push mode using pushing cables for the trip down the Hudson River. In the Lower Bay we switched from pushing ahead to towing astern and off we went.

We towed the Adelaide to Fort Lauderdale, Florida, where the Port Authority was constructing Port Everglades, later to become a major East Coast port. Moran and Atlantic Cement Co. brought most of the cement to construct the Port, which took several years.

After that voyage, I had taken the short trip on the subway to 17 Battery Place, Moran's home office, to pick up my check rather than have them mail it. It was then that I discovered that Marion (Fitzgerald) Daniti was employed there in an adjoining office. It was the first time in a long time that we friends had a chance to talk and catch up. She had healed well from the accident and was substituting as Secretary for Curtis Bay Towing Corp., a Moran subsidiary with a sales office there. We were good friends who shared most of our youth doing things together, so it was fun to get all caught up. I also enjoyed meeting her bosses, Mr. Moore and Wilson.

CHAPTER 17

Coming home after one of the trips in early December, my Mom handed me a letter from the Department of Defense. OMG, I was being drafted into the US Army.... "Your friends and neighbors have selected you ...." I had until the end of the year to activate my Commission in the US Naval Reserve as an Ensign, so I had to get moving. I brought my Cadet blue uniform to a tailor to have my Ensign stripes installed. Then it was off to 90 Church Street in Manhattan to take the Navy physical and thank heavens, I passed it. I also had to fill out many documents to set myself up for receiving my correspondence courses to continue my training as a Naval Officer. On the day that I was to report to 1 Whitehall Plaza to get on the bus to transport me and others to the US Army base in Fort Dix, NJ for Boot Camp, I strode into the Draft Office in my Naval Officer's uniform. "TEN HUT, Officer on deck." Whew, that was close.

I expressed that my goal with Moran was to work on harbor tugs, where you work on so many different type jobs and I could make the required trips for me to take the Pilot's endorsement tests for my license. Their discovery about me was that Kings Point trained me to have exceptional navigational skills, so the

Personnel Department, AKA, Irving Miller, rightly so, sent me on offshore assignments where those skills were most needed.

Moran owned a 20,000 ton capacity bulk barge named the Caribbean that delivered cargoes worldwide. I was called to board the Cathleen Moran, a 3500 HP twin screw ocean going tug for a trip towing the Caribbean from New York to La Ramona, Santa Domingo. There we would load a full load of raw sugar for delivery to Domino Sugar in New York harbor. I was an AB on that trip of 20 days and was told when the Caribbean was empty, we would be returning for a repeat load. It took 10 days to discharge the cargo, so....20 days on, 10 days off...that's ok. Trip two was a repeat, time wise, except I was 2nd Mate on that trip. Trip three was different, starting with me being Chief Mate. The Captain, Lefty Chapman, liked me doing all the navigation chores. Trip three was also very different since we were directed to go to Baltimore to load a full load of grain first, destined for San Juan, Puerto Rico. We were amazed to see the Baltimore grain elevator dump 20,000 tons of grain into the Caribbean in 4 hours flat. The 1600 mile trip to San Juan was uneventful with relatively calm seas and the grain dock was clear so we could start discharging right away. When I inquired as to how long the discharge would take…. shocked would be a good description…19 or 20 days was the estimate. They were going to use two 8" vacuum hoses to unload 20,000 tons of grain!

We were chased away from the discharge dock and directed to go hang on at the Municipal pier in downtown San Juan. We had plenty of time to explore San Juan completely. Condado Beach was where all the large hotels were located, so there were plenty of places to go to pretend you were a tourist having lunches by the pool. My favorite was the San Juan Hyatt, the tallest hotel on the beach with great views from their roof top restaurant. A lot of the crew took advantage of the night life available in San Juan but fortunately we had no bad incidents.

When we were finally discharged, we left Puerto Rico and made the short trip through Mona Pass over to La Ramona to load sugar. One evening at La Romano, I was going ashore to have dinner with our local agent. When I stepped ashore, the pier guard stopped me and gave me a warning. He said, "You are dressed in a red shirt and black pants..... that is the dress of a Communist, you will be stoned." I quickly went back and changed. My Able Bodied seaman on my watch was a US Marine veteran and unlike most of them, this guy was slightly nuts. He'd do things like jumping on the back of a manta ray that swam by the tug, hoping to subdue it, which he didn't. He volunteered to be my body guard for the walk up to my dinner with the agent. While walking up the street, we came upon a small soldier with a rifle, guarding what, I'm not sure. My Marine barked some commands at him and in less than 15 seconds he had the soldier's rifle in pieces on the ground. As we turned to walk away, the soldier says teary eyed… "but I….don't know how to put it back together." I managed to talk my man into re-assembling it.

After 4 days of loading sugar, we were off for New York to a new terminal in Yonkers.. We were gone on that trip for a total of 43 days and when we were freed of the barge and heading back to Moran's yard, we were informed it would only take 3 days to discharge her. I explained to Personnel that 43 days on and 3 days off was not going to cut it and I refused to go. Personnel was not happy.

My next assignment was to tend the coal barges that were coming from Norfolk, VA to feed coal to the big ConEd generator known as "Big Alice" in Astoria, Queens on the East River. I got plenty of use out of my motorcycle and went home every night caked in coal dust. Was Mr. Miller mad at me??

I found myself making excuses to be with Marion more and more. I was not so innocently showing up to get my check right at lunch time so that we could chat once again. Marion and I agreed on so many fronts that it was always a pleasure to have those times together. Also, Misters Moore and Wilson, assumed the roll of matchmakers, encouraging Marion and I to spend time together. At the same time my relation with June was getting more and more strained. She actually said it was my career on the water or no engagement. In addition, Marion was getting pressure from her father because of his justified concerns over my being engaged. I became determined to rectify that situation as soon as possible.

My career at Moran continued with being exposed to the different trades in which they were involved. I was assigned to the Betty Moran as Captain Lefty's mate, towing those same coal barges from Hampton Roads (Norfolk, VA) to "Big Alice" in Astoria, Queens. The Betty never stopped because as you brought a loaded barge to Astoria, an empty one was ready to return to Hampton Roads. The barges were converted WWII Liberty Ships, stripped of engine rooms and deck houses. That lasted for 3 months with 2 weeks on, one week off.

CHAPTER 18

My next orders were to report to Port Richmond and board the Christine Moran at Moran's Yard as Chief Mate. We were outfitting her for a trip estimated to last 20 days or so. The Christine, even though she was only 96' LOA and a had a beam of 25', was a great tug for medium to long trips because she was comfortable in a seaway and very stingy on fuel. She was only 1,000 HP, but with the amount of fuel she carried, she was good for 20+ days at sea, depending on what she was towing.

This job called for us to go to Charleston, SC and pick up two refrigeration barges of approximately 250'x 35', fully loaded with frozen and chilled food for the Sailors and Marines stationed at Roosevelt Roads Naval Station on the East Coast of Puerto Rico. It was a trip of over 1,500 miles and a straight run from Charleston to the Northeast corner of Puerto Rico. We were blessed with light winds and small seas for the entire trip.

One of the deckhands on this trip was a professional fisherman on his time off and he surprised us with what he had brought aboard. When The Chief Engineer notified us that we were in the Gulf Stream, the water temperature jumped significantly, that deckhand broke out his gear. It consisted of a bicycle tire inner tube, a bell, a spool of 100 pound test monofilament fishing line and several large fishing hooks. He ripped up a white tee shirt, attaching a one foot piece to the hook, attached that to the line, let out about 150' of line and attached the other end of the line to the inner tube. He put the inner tube around the after side bitt on the tug and then attached the bell to the inner tube as well. He said all we have to do is wait for the bell to ring. It didn't take long when we heard the bell and ran outside to see a 4' long dolphin (Mahi-Mahi) jumping clear out of the water. Three people started heaving in that line and skipped that fish across the water onto the stern of the Christine. The fish was 40+ pounds. Our cook was overjoyed and he served it to us in many delicious ways.

We arrived at Roosevelt Roads at midnight, having been previously advised that no one would be available to officially accept our arrival until 0800. They did however tell us where we could hang on at a pier to wait until morning. Hauling hawser of a two barge tow isn't fun at night. First, you transfer the 8" hawser from the H-bitt to the gypsey head so you can heave in the main hawser and coil it neatly on deck. When completed, you disconnect it and maneuver to get the first barge made up alongside the tug. We followed the same procedure to get the second barge alongside the other side of the tug. Then we landed alongside the pier and tied up securely to wait. The Naval Officer was very happy with our safe arrival, as their mess hall and PX would soon be full of fresh foods. We spent a couple of hours retrieving our wires and shackles from the barges and properly stowing everything for a safe return to New York.

That we would be heading straight back to New York was a dream. Two days out of Puerto Rico, we were ordered to head back to Charleston, SC to pick up a dead ship (no engine) and tow it to Key Highway Shipyard in Baltimore. The ship was a bulk carrier and was in need of repairs, prior to delivery to her new owners in Canada. We had a nice smooth trip back to Charleston including more fresh fish caught enroute.

They had positioned the ship at the end of their pier, so all we had to do was hook up our hawser and off we went. Smooth sailing ceased when we approached Cape Hatteras, NC. Every sailor is warned about the treachery of passing Cape Hatteras when there is Northeast winds blowing. Northeast winds blowing against 2 to 4 knot currents out of the Southwest makes for some very large standing waves. For 24 hours we never moved one mile forward, all we did was go up and down. As good a sea boat as the Christine was, life in that period was rough. Tilting your mattress to keep yourself in your bunk was not enough. Three ropes were needed: chest, waist and knees to keep you immobile. I could say that you got used to it or more likely you were too exhausted to care.

Eventually the wind and seas calmed and we resumed our trip to Baltimore. Off Key Highway Shipyard, we handed off our tow to our sister company, Curtis Bay Towing of Maryland. We went to Curtis Bay's home pier to properly stow our hawser and wires. We also got fuel and grub for our short trip back to New York. We departed Baltimore and headed for the Chesapeake and Delaware Canal, a shortcut from the upper Chesapeake Bay to the Delaware River. One third of the way into the Canal, we heard an emergency call from a ship that was about one mile ahead of us. The Ship Captain or Pilot was announcing that his ship had lost steering and that he had stopped all forward progress with his ship being held against the rocky North shore of the Canal by a gentle southerly breeze. "I'm going to need a tugboat to help us very quickly," radioed the Captain. I remember getting on the radio saying, "Captain, this is the Moran Towing Corporation's tug Christine Moran and we'll be alongside you to help in 10 minutes." His response, "Holy S***, that's some service." As we approached the ship, I again got on the radio saying, "Captain, the reason you lost steering is that your rudder fell off." The Canal Pilot wisely notified the Canal Dispatcher that there was a large chunk of metal floating in the Canal.

Once we secured our hawser to the ship's bow, we advised her to come dead slow ahead on her main engine. The propeller, without interference of the rudder, would cause the ship's stern to gently lift her off the rocks. We took care of lifting the bow off and we were then underway. I asked the Captain to lock the propeller shaft on his ship and that would provide sufficient drag to keep the ship directly behind us. By this time, orders came down from the ship's agent to tow her up to Philadelphia Shipyard. Once cleared of the Canal by Reedy Island, we headed North. Off Philadelphia Shipyard, we once again turned our tow over, this time to Curtis Bay Towing of Philadelphia. Finally, we were actually heading for our home port. The crew asked if we could turn off the radio telephone, so nothing would interfere with our actually going home.

I was certain that out 30+ days towing around the Southwest Atlantic and East Coast had to be a very profitable time for the little Christine Moran.

CHAPTER 19

My desire to work in the harbor finally happened, although not in the trade I expected. When the SuperSonic Transports (SST's) passenger planes came to be, the plan for New York was to use JFK as the primary terminal. The FAA wisely said you had to have a backup airport in the event of trouble at the primary. Neither LaGuardia nor Newark fit the bill of having a suitable long runway, so they decided to lengthen the main runway at Newark. Great Lakes Dredge Co. devised an ingenious plan to accomplish that task. First, they burrowed a hole horizontally underground from the furthest West berths in Port Elizabeth, under the New Jersey Turnpike and out to fields on the South end of the Airport. A large diameter steel pipe was inserted in that burrowed hole. They then stationed a dredge south of Staten Island near Hoffman Island where there was plenty of clean sand. They used 5,000 cubic yard capacity barges that had to be towed to and from. I wound up on the Barbara Moran, a 1750 HP, diesel electric tug which was one of the class of five tugs that Moran used to up the horsepower race in New York harbor back in the 1950's. She was a fun tugboat to steer and control since she was diesel electric powered and had a very big rudder. We would tow empty barges from Port Elizabeth to the dredge to be put in a loading berth. Then we would make fast in push gear and deliver the loaded scow from the dredge to the discharge unit back in Port Elizabeth. There, they had another ingenious setup using two water jets to turn the sand into a slurry that was easily pumped over to the airport. There were bulldozers and other heavy equipment in those fields to move the sand for the runway construction.

Working on the Barbara entailed working one week on the boat with 4 days off after the first week. Then one week on and 3 days off, all in keeping with the Union contract. I got a lot of trips over the upper bay and Kill Van Kull working towards the 50 round trips required to sit for the first Pilot's license endorsement on my license. I also had some free time to straighten out my personal life.

Breaking an engagement is not a nice or easy thing to do, however June and I grew apart over a lengthy period and that coupled with my growing feelings of wanting to be with Marion made it necessary sooner rather than later. June lived out in Glen Head, Long Island, so I had to borrow Marion's car to get there. It did not go easy. After talking and breaking the engagement, I went out to the car to drive away. June ran out of the house and laid down in front of the car shouting "You should kill me now." I did what I had to do and that was put the car in reverse and backed up the block. Marion and her son Paul came with me and I had dropped them off at a restaurant for lunch. It took a little too long and she was worried and ready to call the police thinking I was shot or something. Like I said: not easy.

It was like a tremendous emotional burden was lifted. Marion and I spent a lot of time going for walks where we thoroughly discussed what we wanted for our future. Walks along Shore Road in Bay Ridge Brooklyn where we lived, overlooking the

Narrows was a favorite spot for us to do just that, plan. Falling deeply in love with Marion came all so easy for me. My Mom had concerns because the Daniti's lived upstairs from her. It turned out not to be of any concern. We loved going out to dinner with Paul coming with us. He was 2 ½ years old and he already was calling me Daddy. We did everything together including going to the World's Fair held in Queens, NY. Marion's Mom was great, often telling us to go out by ourselves while she took care of Paul. I called this writing "an American Dream" and I know falling in love with the most beautiful girl I've ever known is the big part of that dream. The fact that she is smart and cheerful and brings a son who just happens to be my God son for an instant family only enhanced that dream.

With regard to my career at Moran Towing, I explained to Marion that it was important for me, that when I look for a shore job, that I do it as Captain McVay and not as Mr. Mate. It would have a tremendous effect on where I would wind up and how much money I could make. She knew that all along and did everything to help me achieve that goal.

Remember that ship that we towed with the Christine Moran to Baltimore's Key Highway Shipyard; it had been refurbished and was ready to go to her new owners.

I got the call to join the Diana Moran at the yard. The Diana was relatively new, 105'LOA, was rated at 1750 HP and was equipped with a towing machine. The quarters made her a comfortable boat. We ran light down to Key Highway in Baltimore and were handed the tow by Curtis Bay tugs. This ship, a bulker, was not that large so we took her out via the Chesapeake & Delaware Canal then down the Delaware River to the Ocean. Our tow was bound for Seven Islands, Quebec at the mouth of the St. Lawrence River's North shore. We ran into rough weather off the Grand Banks, but the real surprise was having to detour around ice flows that came out of the St. Lawrence River. It was a 75 mile detour before we could get back on track towards Seven Islands. Our arrival was made easier when Canadian tugs came out of the port and relieved us of our charge. We amazingly went back to New York without a hitch. Our route back took us through the Cape Cod Canal, a place with lots of childhood memories. Then on through Buzzard's Bay, Block Island Sound, The Race and on down Long Island Sound where I had so many sailing memories.

Old Captain Sven on the SS Flying Fish asked me why I would want to work on a little piece of shit like a tugboat. The more I did it, the more I loved it. With your hands on the throttle(s) and the steering wheel and using your 800+ tons displacement to push other things around much bigger than you, was a thrill. Going up on a ship's bridge wing, at sea, for a week or more, hoping to see something other than ocean was incomparable to constantly doing something different each watch.

I was assigned as Chief Mate to the Harriet to tow dredging

equipment to Nassau in the Bahamas. Off Fort Pierce, FL, our hawser got snagged on a wreck somehow and when the Captain made the mistake of backing down on the hawser, in no time, it was wrapped around the propeller shaft and snapped. Since the tow was secured to the wreck on the bottom, the Captain decided to go into Ft. Pierce and seek help. There was no help available. I always brought my mask and snorkel with me on trips, especially heading for warm water. I decided to go down and take a look. There were three hard wraps of 9" nylon hawser around the shaft, a situation I thought I could fix. With hacksaw in hand, I began sawing the line. This was, take a breath, dive down 12' or so, saw like crazy, then back up another breath. It was exhausting work and took me 5 hours to finally free the shaft of rope. On one dive, I had this spooky feeling that something big was behind me. I turned, only to see three dolphins looking at me working. Eerie! That dredging equipment transformed the Eastern end of Nassau Island into a paradise of luxury hotels like Atlantis, and gorgeous beaches.

When I got back and saw Captain Goodwin, VP Operations, in the office, he said he's going to put a gold star on my record for a nice job. I said to him: "I'd be happy to trade a gold star for 5 hours OT for going above and beyond." He laughed and agreed. That was my first meeting with Captain Goodwin.

CHAPTER 20

I had been assigned to almost every tug that Moran operated out of the New York division. It got so I could tell which tug was which at night, just by the configuration of the running lights and deck lights. This was the job and this was the business for me. I loved it.

The two week on, one week off routine didn't leave me with as much time as I longed for to be with Marion. As much as I loved the job, the love that was growing in me for Marion was all consuming, so being away was very difficult. The offshore trips that seemed to come my way most often, had totally unpredictable schedules and that was worse. Marion was working full time in the Sales Office for Curtis Bay Towing for Mr. Wilson and Mr. Moore. They would often tell Marion that when I showed up to ostensibly to pick up my check, to just go. It was Mr. Moore who said that, which sometimes infuriated Mr. Wilson who had a Sales agreement to get out that day. We loved the time together.

Going out and back on those voyages was slowly giving me the fifty round trips required to sit for my initial New York harbor Pilot's endorsement. I chose taking the test for Kill Van Kull, the body of water encompassing St. George, Staten Island to Norton's

Point in New Jersey where there was a hard right turn into the entrance to Newark Bay. It was a short piece of navigation but was perfect for the initiation to get the Pilot's endorsement to my Third Mate's license earned at Kings Point. The test required answering a battery of questions on the Rules of the Road, basic seamanship and pollution prevention. After that, you had to draw the chart from memory including all aids to navigation like buoys, a lighthouse, range lights, beacons and water depths. The reward was....

"FIRST CLASS PILOT OF STEAM AND MOTOR VESSELS OF ANY GROSS TONS UPON: Kill Van Kull from St. George, Staten Island to Norton's Point." I received the ANY GROSS TONS because that was the highest tonnage rating already on my Third Mate's license. I was very proud to get that extra endorsement on my license as my first step to matching my father's license and my grandfather's and my uncles, etc., etc. By the way.... Kill Van Kull was and is one of the most traveled ship routes in New York Harbor, so it was an important piece to have added to my license. Moran's shipyard was on the Kill as well. The name is a leftover from the first Dutch settlement of New York.

It happened that I did get the opportunity to work on a "Day Boat." These were the premier jobs to have in Moran's New York tug operation. The crew consisted of one Captain, who happened to be a Docking Master as well, one Mate, one deckhand, one Engineer and a cook. The crew was expected to work twelve hours per day, above which was overtime pay. The Docking Master did several dockings and undockings per day during which time the mate handled the tug. It happened that day for me because the Martha Moran's mate did not make it to work and I was aboard the Kerry Moran hanging on at Moran's yard between jobs. At 0500, I was contacted and asked to switch over to the Martha and report to Captain Whitey Mattsson, the Docking Pilot. He informed me that we should go to Esso Constable Hook, NJ, to get fuel, and then go over to 69th Street, Brooklyn and pick up another pilot. The Martha was one of the last "bell boats" in the Moran New York fleet. You will recall that bell boats do not have pilothouse engine controls and the Engineer is stationed in the upper engine room waiting for bells, gongs or jingles from the pilothouse to give the proper engine response. Whitey never even asked me if I knew the signals, so it was fortunate that I still remembered them from when I summered with my Dad, nine years before. Everything worked out well except that while transiting the 30 minutes jaunt to get over to Brooklyn, the engineer fell asleep at the controls. After numerous unanswered bells to "stop," I set the wheel to halfway to starboard, to make a giant circle, and then ran below to wake him. I did not want to sound the general alarm on my first day aboard.

Whitey Mattsson was very interesting individual and a nice guy to boot. He raised horses on his farm in upstate Florida, NY to specifically race as trotters at betting tracks. Whitey was a gambler as well, betting on all sorts of things. My second day with him found us being called out at 0550 in the morning and to report to the pier at 55th street Brooklyn and to pick up cargo scow number 55 for a delivery to a ship. Whitey bet the "numbers" and found the longshoreman with whom he could place the bet ….naturally for 555. He asked me to join him, but I was never into gambling at all. Stupid me…number 555 paid $1200.00 for his $10.00 bet. Whitey was an accurate nickname for this Scandinavian. His skin was almost transparent it was so white as well as his hair. My assignment on the Martha only lasted for two days and then I was out to sea again. I did however, get a good taste of how exciting it would be to be a Docking Master.

Marion and I's relationship was so certain that on Mother's Day, May 9th, we officially became engaged to be married. Marion's Mom was very happy because she really liked me and at one time actually said to me, "You are going to marry one of my daughters no matter what." Her prophesy was fulfilled! We spent as much time together as our jobs permitted. One of the fun things we did was extensive house hunting. We were fulfilling the dream of so many young couples from New York City: "get married and buy a house, out on the Island" (Long Island). We spent many weekends searching for what would fit us and our family plans and one we could actually afford. We did it for months, finally deciding on Smithtown, LI. Normally, if I had a nine to five, Monday through Friday job in New York City, Smithtown would be an awfully long daily commute on the Long Island RR. With my sporadic schedule though, that was not as much of a problem. Marion was going to quit working at Curtis Bay, getting back to taking care of Paul full time, since her Mom would not be in the picture once we moved.

An interesting thing happened to Marion at work. One morning, shortly after arriving, Mr. Moore and Mr. Wilson were in the office when a secretary came in with a note saying: "Admiral Edmond J. Moran would like to speak to Marion." Panic. What could that be about??? So, she went down to the big corner office of the Chairman of the Board of Moran and sat down in front of the giant desk and waited............. "So, I understand that you are going to marry one of my officers," said the Admiral. He wanted to know all about her and me, where we lived and what were our plans. The conversation was mostly about her, but she recalls he did mention Kings Point and me. It was all very cordial. Moore and Wilson had to know every word that was spoken because interaction with Admiral was truly rare.

The Admiral was a true WWII war hero and a good friend

of General then President Dwight Eisenhower. He put together the artificial harbor built at Normandy in France that allowed the discharging of supplies which made the Normandy invasion feasible.. He implemented it using commandeered tugboats from the New York Harbor tug companies.

The head of tug personnel, Irving Miller, probably got tired of hearing me talk about working in the harbor rather than these long offshore adventures. I don't know if it was his idea of a joke, but he assigned me to the newly acquired "garbage" run. Each and every day, New Yorkers dumped approximately 26,000 tons of garbage for disposal. Garbage trucks in each of the four boroughs (Brooklyn, Queens, Manhattan and the Bronx) would dump their refuse into barges placed in one of nine different piers located throughout the City. The barges would then be towed to the massive dump site located on Staten Island at Fresh Kills. Staten Island garbage was trucked directly with no barges necessary. It was a good contract for Moran to get because it kept five tugs going steadily. The work was steady and so was the stink. There was so much unmanned barge handling that four deckhands were assigned to each tug, two to a watch. Once you got used to the odor and the flies, the work was fairly simple. I did several 2 week on, 1 week off stints.

Marion's sister Evelyn married Steve Carbone, a local Bay Ridge Brooklyn fellow who I knew of from mutual acquaintances, but I didn't really KNOW him. They were married on August 8, 1964. Steve grew up in different parts of Brooklyn but his family eventually settled in a house on 88th street. I grew up near 92nd Street, but in Brooklyn, where each city block was like its own separate town, four blocks away was remote. That was especially true if you did not attend the same grammar schools. It was the Fitzgeralds who brought us together as great friends.

Jack and Carol, Steve and Evelyn and Marion and I became best friends and that carried over to all of our kids.

Marion and I wanted to set the date for our wedding and we came up with September 18th, a date where we could reserve both St. Anselm's Church and the Officer's Club in Fort Hamilton Army Base right there in Bay Ridge Brooklyn. My being a US Naval Reserve Officer qualified us to reserve the Club for our wedding.

That summer of 1965, Jack and Carol were house hunting as well. Jack was a New York City Policeman and the South Shore Long Island RR schedules were more compatible to his schedules. Their efforts wound up with them buying a house in Babylon near the South Shore.

The split ranch house we settled on in Smithtown was a beauty with three bedrooms, the kitchen, living room and dining room upstairs and a fourth bedroom plus a den downstairs. There was also a two car garage downstairs, all for $18,990.00. Our mortgage payment was $135.00/month, but remember in 1965, if you were making $7,000 or 8,000/ year, you were living pretty well. Our sales agreement was a bit unique with two individuals buying the house rather than a married couple. We'd straighten that out after our wedding. Every bit of free time we had, found us out in Smithtown prepping the house for our occupancy after September 18th. I painted out the two car garage and Marion organized the kitchen and we took delivery of everything else like furniture and fixtures prior to our moving. From the outset of our marriage, Marion and I always outfitted our houses to be a comfortable place for people, especially relatives, to come and visit. Looking back on that time, it was a terrific experience. An added dividend was that Jack and Carol's place was only thirty minutes away.

Irving Miller called me one day in August telling me that this wonderful trip was booked for the Christine Moran and he thought that I would be the best choice to fill the Chief Mate's billet for that trip. The Christine was going to pick up two reefer barges in Norfolk, VA and tow them to Saigon, Vietnam. A quick mental calculation on my part showed that trip to be one of six or seven months duration. I told Mr. Miller to please take a walk over to Curtis Bay Towing's Sales office and that there was a beautiful blonde in that office and tell her that you are about to send me off on a six month trip. He was actually annoyed that I was refusing. "I'M GETTING MARRIED NEXT MONTH!!!" I said in a raised voice. I didn't go obviously and the trip actually lasted close to nine months.

CHAPTER 21

September 18th finally came and it was a beautiful weather day as hoped. Our wedding was a smaller affair with only close family and friends in attendance. It started with my Best Man, Donald, collecting $10.00 from me for a bet I had with him saying that I would not get married before I was 25 years old. It was a bet that I was happy to lose at age 23.

There was a population explosion to be seen there as well. My brother's wife Cathy was pregnant. Jack Fitzgerald's wife Carol was pregnant and Steve Carbone's wife Evelyn was pregnant. My sister Edith was also pregnant, but she and her husband Joe were living in Savannah, GA where NOAA had stationed him. Her pregnancy and his being out to sea precluded any travel to our wedding. When the priest found out that I was young Paul's Godfather, he said to me: "Russ, aren't you taking this Godfather thing a bit too seriously?"

It was so nice to see everyone who attended, some people we haven't seen in a while. It was not a super fancy wedding with gowns and tuxes and that was the way we both wanted it. It did not take away from my own feelings as to how lucky I am. Marrying the most beautiful woman (inside and out) I know, who also happens to be my best friend and on top of that, we have a ready made family with the addition of Paul. Having the ceremony at the beautiful St., Anselm's Church, Marion's Parish, added an aura of reverence and authenticity that we both wanted.

The US Army's Fort Hamilton Officer's Club could not be beat for having our wedding reception. It sat on a hill overlooking the Narrows (of rafting fame) right under the newly constructed Verranzano Bridge, spanning from Brooklyn to Staten

Island. Even with its panoramic styled windows, the Club still felt intimate enough for our smaller group of about 25. The only one not happy was Steve Carbone who spent most of the time downstairs watching "Mickey Mantle Day" on television. Yankee fans...Ugh!!

The food and drinks were excellent. We left plenty of time for us to mingle with those relatives who we rarely see and those we often see. Marion's ex-boss Mr. Wilson was there. When it was time, Marion and I left to go to her parents house, pick up our luggage and head off to Motel on a Mountain upstate in Suffren, NY. We drove all the way up to the George Washington Bridge when Marion realized that she left some clothes and personal items back home. In the spirit of no arguments on our wedding day, we backtracked to Brooklyn to pick them up. We were scheduled to stay for four days on our honeymoon.

All we could think of was that beautiful house waiting for us back in Smithtown. We cut the honeymoon short after a day and a half and took off for Smithtown Long Island, never telling anyone. Looking back…....I named this book "an American Dream" and here I was married to the most beautiful woman I could ever hope for who was also my best friend, starting our life in a brand new home of our own……..who could ask for more? Not me!!

It wasn't long after we were home that Marion wanted to go to Brooklyn to pick up Paul at her Mom's house. Before we actually left, we had to hide because Jack and Carol showed up and put a big redwood picnic table in our back yard. That was their surprise wedding gift to us and we didn't want to spoil it.

We did go back to Brooklyn to pick up Paul. It was not a happy day for Marion's Mom Mae, because she had come to really love taking care of Paul. He was a happy kid and easy going, so the transition out to a new house created no issues whatsoever. And Marion was overjoyed to have our little family settled. We lived at 25 Ramondo Lane and the families who moved in near us as each house was completed turned out to be great group of people. They were also helpful to Marion when I was away on a tug voyage. Marion, being so self sufficient, rarely needed help, but it was nice being in a neighborhood of friendly folks. Often, when I was gone, Marion's family would come out to visit, as it was a pleasant escape from the City.

As for Moran, I continued getting exposed to all of their varied operations coming out of the New York office. Work was steady and I tried to keep my time on vs. time off to the two for one as much as possible. Being off for several days at a time was good for getting projects done around the house. It was also good for taking mini trips when the weather cooperated. We did a lot with Jack and Carol also, like backyard fun or going to local parks. We got together with Evelyn and Steve as well, when they would make the trip out from Brooklyn where they lived. My brother Don and his growing family moved a lot as did Edith and Joe. Visits with them would have to be overnighters or more, so they were less frequent.

During that winter of 1965/66, I made many coastwise and ocean going trips, but there was one that stood out from all the rest. It was a rescue trip to remember, because you always remember those times when you came too close to becoming a tragedy. I can look back on it with some bravado because we survived. I wrote a story about that trip that caught the eye of the Editor of Moran's Towline magazine, who then included it in an edition of the Magazine. I am including that article as written.

CHAPTER 22
To the Limit

*From an Era Before High-Tech Met the
High Seas, a Tugboatman's Story*

By Capt. Russ McVay

On a cold February night in 1966, at around midnight, a ringing telephone in our home awakened my wife and me. The call was from my office; I worked for Moran Towing as a Mate on tugs. I was 24 years old. I was told to get to Moran's yard in Staten Island as soon as possible, to board the *Cathleen Moran* for a rescue mission: Meyer Line, a Norwegian shipping company, had a ship — the *MV Havlom* — that was wallowing in heavy seas after losing her rudder. She was 120 miles East of St. Johns, Newfoundland. Conditions were too rough to jury-rig a rudder, and the mariners were afraid that the farther offshore the ship drifted, the more the danger of capsizing.

My wife asked how long I'd be gone; I estimated three days up there and seven days to tow the ship back to New York. I told her to call the office in about ten days to get an idea of when I would be back.

After a speedy drive to Port Richmond, Staten Island, I joined the *Cathleen*'s crew and we spent the next eight hours lashing down the main hawser and loading supplies. These included a spare hawser; 2,000 feet of 10-inch nylon; grub; 10 sheets of one-inch marine plywood; and spare shackles. The task was accomplished using the entire crew of ten: the captain and two mates, three able-bodied seamen, three engineers and one cook. We were to stand two four-hour watches per day, the same as aboard a ship. We also put aboard a line-throwing–50-caliber rifle instead of the usual Lyle gun. The *Cathleen* did not have a towing winch with wire.

The plan was to get to St. Johns as quickly as possible, top-off fuel, and head out for the *Havlom*. It took us three-plus days to get there, because the weather was not cooperating; we ran into high winds and seas. It was especially rough after we came out of the north end of the Cape Cod Canal. A week before we got to St. Johns, the area had gotten eight feet of snow dropped on it. We pulled into the fuel dock and found our 10" x 2,000' main hawser frozen solid and looking like a rat's nest on the stern. It took five hours of every man in the crew working to soften that line up with warm water before we could re-stow it up on the boat deck. Moving it was critical — the seas crashing across the stern were too much for even the strongest lashings to keep it in place. There was so much snow that the dock master had to use a sextant, getting angles off building corners, to pinpoint where to start digging to find fuel valves buried under drifts. We were finally able to top off our fuel tanks.

When all was prepared, I borrowed the dockman's snowshoes and trudged up to the office to get the latest position of our quarry. When the office relayed the latitude and longitude of the *Havlom*, I was aghast: it wasn't 120 miles east of Newfoundland; it was *1,200* miles East, and being blown farther still by 50- to 80-knot westerly winds. As we passed out of the breakwater of St. Johns harbor, we met a large gray vessel inbound. We talked; it was the Canadian Coast Guard ocean station weather vessel. She was inbound due to conditions that made it too rough for her to stay on station. 80-knot winds and 55-foot seas will do that. And there we were, outbound… Yet we knew that a ship might sink with all hands if we didn't help, and we set sail.

Have you ever been on a small boat moving along with a following sea? The waves lift the stern and it's like you are surfing down the front of the wave, accelerating. Doing that on a 105-foot, 3,500 HP, twin screw boat displacing more than 700 tons is the thrill of a lifetime — if scariness is your idea of a thrill — and it's exhausting. Between the AB and myself, we did one-half-hour on, one-half-hour off. It was too rough to use the autopilot, so we had to hand steer to prevent a broach, which would have certainly caused a rollover. When the stern lifted it would bring the two 11-foot propellers out of the water, and the tug would rattle like a freight train until they caught the wave again and shot you down the front. You had to fight the vibrating wheel on the way down, making adjustments to keep the stern directly perpendicular to the wave. When you reached the bottom of the trough, green water would be propelled onto and over the pilot house windows. The propellers would dig in again, their vibration feeling like it would rattle your teeth out as the tug tried to rid itself of tons of water, and then the stern would lift again. At the end of the four-hour watch, we were beat. If we were to find the ship, we'd be turning around and going right back into this roaring mess with her.

While the wind induced waves, distant storms induced

swells, creating huge and confused seas that threw the tug about so jarringly that sleep was next to impossible. You would get into bed — a bunk that was basically a steel pipe rack — and then tie three lines through the pipe sides: one at the ankles, one at the waist and a final one at the chest. Without these restraints you'd be guaranteed of getting tossed out of your bunk.

I remember that the cook had a very difficult time trying to do his job. So many meals were started only to wind up as slop, with pots thrown around on the top of the stove. One morning, the fellow was determined to cook eggs for us. After two sets of fried eggs wound up flipping out of the pan and sliding down the bulkhead. He gave up; it would be dry cereal for all.

This is all pre-GPS; the best we could do was to try to get a noon sun line to help with the navigation. I was out in front of the pilot house, feet jammed up to the railing, stopwatch in one hand, sextant in the other, trying to find the horizon from a 26-foot height of eye in 50-foot seas — dead reckoning at best. They didn't teach *this* at Kings Point.

When we got close to where we thought the ship would be we tried to activate our Radio Direction Finder (RDF). We had told the *Havlom* to broadcast a signal at 2182, so we could home in on her. But our antenna was broken from the foul weather, so we reversed it, sending out a signal that would enable the ship to home in on *us*. We didn't have satellite radios back then, but we did have single sideband radios that allowed us to talk to our own office. The *Havlom* could use its sidebands to radio its position and the reciprocal course to our signal to its home office, which would call our office, which would in turn call us.

After a day of maneuvering around trying to find the ship, we were in a weather situation with a very low ceiling and cloud cover. We were actually close enough to contact the *Havlom* via VHF, and we told its crew to aim all their deck lights up and turn them on at exactly 2100 hours. At 2100 we scanned the horizon, saw a glow on the low clouds, and raced toward it.

At about this time, my wife called the office to get an idea of when I would return. It had been ten days, after all. The dispatcher at Moran laughed at her inquiry and told her, "Your husband is now off the coast of Ireland."

As daybreak emerged, we were greeted with a cheering ship's crew, happy that we were there. The wind was so strong that the tops of the waves were being blown off as spume. With our deck gang about to start working, we released a little oil into the water to try to calm it down a bit. The net effect of that move was to create an even more slippery deck, and we almost lost one of the ABs overboard.

We explained to the *Havlom*'s Captain how the tow was going to be rigged: He was told to "hang off" his port anchor — i.e., to run several parts of one-half-inch wire from the anchor shackle to the nearest bit, have the crew secure the anchor in the hawsepipe, and then disconnect the patent link of the anchor chain and run the chain through the "bullnose" (for you engineers, that's the forward-most fairlead at the stem). The ship's crew was to let out about a one-half-shot (45 feet) and bring the end of the chain back on deck over the rail. We used the line-throwing gun to get our hawser over to the ship. The projectile was attached to 600 feet of string, which was attached to 600 feet of half-inch line, which was attached to 600 feet of 3-inch painter that was used to haul the hawser aboard. This was done successfully, and our hawser was connected to the ship's anchor chain.

After the *Havlom* let out another four shots of chain (360 feet), we were ready to begin the tow. The idea was to add extra weight to the catenary curve of the towline, and to avoid chafing worries at the bullnose. Our 10-inch nylon hawser was like a rubber band, and with the anchor chain, we were not worried about breaking the towline. On the tug end, we used a long-enough piece of anchor chain from the "H" bit aft to clear the stern rail and alleviate the worry of chafing.

Given our position close to Ireland, we thought for sure we'd be towing the *Havlom* to Southampton or some other repair facility in the U.K. When we were told to head for New York because all the ship's cargo was needed there, it was heartbreaking. At least at this juncture we had the superior navigation capabilities of the ship, and would be able to steer a better course for home. But in the first 24 hours of heading directly back into turbulent seas, we went exactly 25 miles. At this rate, we'd run out of fuel before we got halfway there.

You had to hand it to the Moran's chief engineer and his assistants. The company's offshore tugs were designed with plenty of fuel tanks; when one tank emptied, it would be filled with seawater and sealed off. This maintained the stability needed in rough seas. With the crew keeping track of these adjustments, the *Cathleen*'s engines ran smoothly.

Conversing with the *Havlom*'s captain, we decided that since he had lost his rudder but still had power to his propeller, he should turn the ship's propeller over at 10 revolutions to take some of the strain off the towline. With that assist, we got up to four knots. We then told him to increase to 15 RPM and hold it there, which boosted our progress to over 120 miles a day. For several days, this configuration produced excellent results.

One evening, I went to the bridge to relieve the watch a few minutes early, so I could get my eyes used to the dark. In very rough conditions, you would wait until the tug got to the top of a wave, take a quick look around for traffic, and then drop down into the trough to wait for the next crest. On one crest, I looked to the starboard and saw a ship's running lights. I told the mate that we had traffic nearby, but he didn't see it, so we waited for the next crest. Sure enough, there was a ship to starboard. The thought dawned on us, "Oh my God, that's our tow." I quickly radioed the *Havlom* and asked how many revolutions they were doing. The ship's mate proudly offered that he had got her up to 62 revolutions. She was passing us! The hawser became taut, and with the ship right on our starboard beam, the forces involved laid the tug over almost 90 degrees–right, over a cresting, confused sea. The aquatic impact blew out all the windows on the starboard side of the wheelhouse, not to mention the inch-and-a-half solid oak door on the boat deck. Green water came pouring through the openings, sloshing down the companionway to the main deck interior. Crew members came running out of their rooms with life jackets on, screaming that we were going to die.

When we righted, we were being dragged stern first until the ship shut down her engine and came to a stop. The General Alarm was sounded, though it was ultimately not needed. It was February. It was night. We were freezing, exhausted and scared.

It soon became apparent that we were not sinking, and we still had engines and generators. But we needed to move quickly to board up the broken windows and door. Thank heavens it was standard procedure to stock up on sheets of marine plywood; we had put them aboard back at the Moran yard. By daybreak, we were ready to go again. There was no use in screaming at the ship's captain at this point, but it was made perfectly clear that 15 RPM means 15 RPM.

There was no letup in the weather, but our hopes to be diverted to Halifax never materialized, so we continued on to New York. After 23 days of living hell — lashing seas, cold food, a near capsizing and utter exhaustion — we sailed into New York Harbor under the Verrazano Bridge. The Bridge never looked more beautiful. When we disconnected from the *Havlom*, the ship's entire crew assembled on deck and gave us a roaring cheer of gratitude.

We brought the mighty *Cathleen* back to the yard, where she had to undergo about $60,000 worth of repairs — about $432,000 in today's dollars. Later, the management of Meyer Line sent a check for $1,500 to each of us crew members, with hearty thanks for saving their ship.

I was thankful that I got to experience this when I was so young, because it was an experience that served me well when I went on to fleet operations management later in my career. And it was now obvious to me that the thought behind the design and construction of Moran's offshore tugs was gleaned from highly seasoned mariners with decades of experience — people who knew how to prepare for all eventualities because they had first-hand knowledge of what those eventualities were. Their wisdom had been instrumental in keeping us alive and getting the job done.

Havlom 1961 Lubecker Flenderwerke, P.Meyer-Oslo-1

CHAPTER 23

After that 23 day rescue trip, in February, in the North Atlantic Ocean, I began to yearn for an alternative. I had not increased the Pilotage endorsements on my license and more importantly, I was away from home too, too much. Additionally, I knew that I could do anything that they threw my way regarding offshore trips, so I kept an eye open for that something different.

I was assigned to the Patricia Moran which was working in the harbor and after several days, we were standing by at Moran's yard waiting for an upcoming job. I had received a call from the Personnel Department notifying me to switch over to the Martha Moran whenever we were near each other, to cover for someone sick. I was able to do that late that night. That next morning at about 0500, the Patricia backed out of the Yard, only to have the small tankship, the Morania Marlin, ram her broadside. The Patricia was hung up on the Marlin's bow, then pushed across the channel colliding with the inbound Diana Moran pushing a coal barge. All this happened so fast and with the Patricia's hull penetrated in the engine room, she sunk quickly, killing all hands aboard. It should not have happened. The Marlin should never have been running in the dark, so close to the pier heads of three very busy Yards: Moran, then Reinauer and Caddel's Shipyard. What a disaster!

Marion's Dad, Gerry Hession, heard of a Moran tug sinking in a short news flash on the radio and having spoken to Marion earlier, he thought she mentioned that I was on the Patricia. He casually called Marion again asking among other things, what tug was Russ on? Marion knew I reported to the Patricia, but I never got to tell her of the switch. He never said a thing and then he called Moran's office, but they were apparently instructed to say nothing to any inquiries. Gerry and May drove out to Smithtown fearing "this cannot happen to Marion again."

My friend, Tom Sullivan, home from the SS Flying Fish, also heard the radio report and he also called Marion ostensibly to just say hello and inquired as to what tug I was on. He later said he was ready to come to our house to offer support.

The Martha was very busy that morning, so it was awhile before I could get to the phone. At about 0900 the opportunity presented itself to call and by then everybody was so relieved that I was not on the Patricia. It was very sad to contemplate the loss of friends, alongside of whom I just worked. To this day, whenever I think of the sad Patricia incident, I have to feel that someone was watching over me. It was my miracle. Thank you God.

We found out that Marion was pregnant in late January, with a due date anticipated for October. That raised the level of excitement at our house with setting up a nursery bedroom and getting Paul ready to have a new baby brother or sister. We actually bought a bunk bed set up for Paul's room with guard rails on the bottom so Paul, at 3 years old, was safe.

At one point in September, the tug I was on, was tied up near an Esso tug at a fuel dock. I inquired into their working schedules and thought that their one week on and one week off sounded like something I would love. I got the telephone number for their

Personnel Department. Mr. Chuck Sheelan was their Personnel Manager with an office in Bayonne, NJ, so I called him. He requested that I prepare a resume and set up a meeting, something I really did not expect. Jobs on the oil company's equipment were treasured assignments and the seamen who got them, never left; they were that valuable. Equal pay scales with the union tugs in the harbor, equal time with a week on and off and no strikes. The reason why the oil companies like Esso, Texaco and Mobil kept their own fleets of harbor tugs, barges and small tankers, was in case the union tugs went out on strike. With their own equipment they would have no interruption of service. Those Esso vessels insured that their distribution from their refinery in Bayway, NJ and their large tank farm at Constable Hook in Bayonne, NJ, would not cease.

Also, the arrivals and departures of their large ships bringing crude oil to their refinery would not be impeded. It was all because Local 333, United Marine Division had a long history of going out on prolonged strikes. 333 was a strong Union because of the backing of the International Longshoreman's Association (ILA stevedores), their affiliated Union. The Longshoremen would not load or unload ships unless they were docked and undocked by Local 333 tugs. The ILA had no leverage like that over the oil companies. I thought my meeting went well with Mr. Sheelan and was left only with: "I'll let you know."

There is a subject that I need to bring up at this point. There came a day while working for Moran that I got a call to come to the Union office for a meeting with Capt. Joseph O'Hare, the Union President and Willard Quick, the Union Financial Officer. Captain O'Hare reminded me that the Union gave me a $1,000.00 scholarship when I entered the Academy and now he wanted me to do him a favor. He said that in the old days, when he sat down to negotiate a new contract between the owners and his Union, he was dealing with the "old time" owners, who ran tugs themselves when they were young. Today, his adversaries across the table were "hot shot" college types and that presented problems for him. His proposal was for me to run for office in the next Union election for the post of delegate. Delegates sat at the negotiation table for the Union. I asked, "What if I run and don't win?" "Oh! Don't worry, you'll win!" After much discussion, it was left that I would think about it and let them know.

I already knew that this path was not what I had in mind for my career. My father had been a delegate for one year and quit. My Mom told me he was disgusted with the corruption and couldn't take it any longer. "Oh don't worry, you'll win" was just the type of thing that my Dad nor I could stomach. I turned them down.

Two wonderful things happened in the middle of October. The first and most important thing was the birth of a beautiful healthy boy, born on the 14th, who for the longest time was going to be named Kevin Patrick, but on the last minute was changed to Scott Michael. Because of the auto accident where Marion suffered multiple fractures of her pelvis, Scott was born via C-section that required a longer hospital stay. Marion's Mom and Dad came out to help and it was a good thing, since I was called to return to work.

But, before I left, I was able to tell Marion that Esso called and they offered me a job on their harbor tugs. The offer was to be a deckhand and the pay was only $750.00 per month. Mr. Sheelan encouraged me, saying several of the Captains and Mates were approaching retirement, so it wouldn't be too long before I could get a Mates job. Getting only $750.00/mo was going to make things very tight for us but the thought of that extra time at home made it impossible to refuse.

My first assignment was as deckhand on the Esso New Jersey, which happened to be the sister tug of the Christine Moran, a boat with which I was very familiar. The skipper, Captain Ken Krieger and I hit it off right away and he let me handle the boat for our entire watches except when I had to be on deck. Captain Ken was also one of the extra Docking Masters for Esso and as such would leave the tug to pilot Esso tankships through the harbor and safely put them into their berth. There were two Esso tugboats in New York harbor, the Esso New Jersey and the Esso Massachusetts. The "Mass" was bigger all around and considered their No. 1 tugboat in the fleet. In addition, the fleet also included two tug/barge units, the Esso Pelham and the Esso Maryland. They also operated a small tanker, the Esso Hudson. Those last three units were crucial to the distribution system for the New York/New Jersey division.

Having all that extra time off allowed me to pursue adding Pilotage endorsements to my license. I discovered that if you took the Coast Guard Pilotage exams every 30 days, after the first one, you would not have to take Rules of the Road, Pollution Prevention, etc., just draw the chart from memory. I equipped the extra bedroom downstairs in our house with a draftsman's table like I had when working as a draftsman for Con Edison. My efforts paid off and since the additional endorsements only required 15 round trips, I was ready to do the whole harbor and tributaries. The most complicated was New York Harbor, Lower bay with its 105 aids to navigation. There were multiple channels with their own markers in the area from the Verranzano Bridge out to Ambrose Light and from Coney Island on the East to the Raritan River on the West. Additionally, I had sufficient time on my license to sit for my Masters license with limited tonnage that covered any tug in the Esso fleet or any tug for that matter. I was officially Captain Russ McVay for which I had planned and that was good.

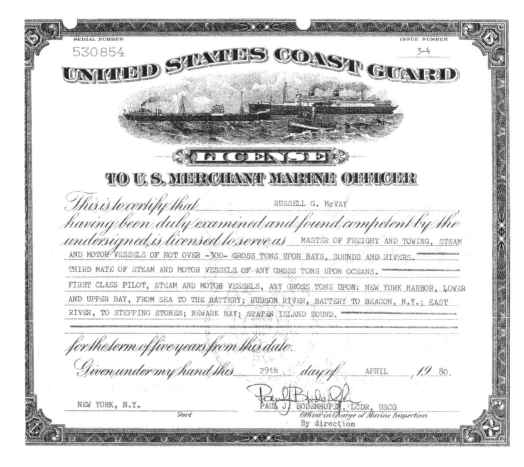

Two months into my assignment on the New Jersey, one of the Captains on the Massachusetts retired. That meant another mate got bumped up to Captain, and a position as Mate was given to me, luckily under Captain Ken. My mentor was also nice enough to take me up on ships while he was Piloting and when I was off watch on the tug.

We did work twelve hours per day, 6 hours on and 6 off, so

there were plenty of opportunities to ride ships with Ken. He eventually let me do some of the ship piloting myself, with him of course right there observing. He also taught me many tricks on how to handle the Esso barges.

In January of 1967, a new Manager of the Esso Marine Department was appointed, Mr. Al Giallorenzi. One of his first instructions for "his" Department, was if you were a Captain or Mate on any vessel operated by Esso, you needed to have the license to cover that job. These were uninspected towing vessels so the license requirements were vague. It came to pass that at the same time when that was enacted, one of the shore side Docking Pilots retired. Captain Neilsen of the Massachusetts was selected to take his place as a shore side Pilot, leaving his job open for an officer in the fleet with a Master's license. In the entire New York Esso fleet, most Captains and Mates only had a small piece of Pilotage on their licenses with no Captain's license, everyone except ME. There I was at age 25, Captain of the Number 1 tug in New York harbor for Esso and now making $1,000.00 per month. There was a saying back then among my peers: "If I only made $10,000.00 per year, we would live like kings." I reported to the Massachusetts for the first time and found that the youngest crew member aboard was my deckhand who was 55 years old. When we were introduced, his first remark was, "It's going to be very hard to refer to you as The Old Man." I said: "Call me Russ and that will be fine."

The Esso Massachusetts was a fun boat to handle, she was single screw, 1600 HP, displaced 700 tons, had diesel electric propulsion and a rudder like a barn door. Having had a good education in the laws of Physics, I would learn to do tricks with that tugboat. It was fun to be at work and Captain Ken still got me up on ships to learn piloting when possible. I learned about bank cushions when steering a deeply laden ship in a vertical walled dredged channel and becoming more cognizant of tidal depths, currents and calculating each to use to your advantage. It was a thoroughly enjoyable experience and on top of that, crew change day was every Tuesday at noon, a far cry from the erratic schedules at Moran.

My crew consisted of my Mate, two deckhands, a Chief Engineer, an Asst. Engineer and a cook. Did we get lucky with our cook, Ray Tavares, because he would spoil us. After getting aboard he would for instance, come up to me asking if we had time, please go up to the Fulton Fish Market. I always made time if possible and Ray would go up the street and come back with things like a bushel of clams (600) and plenty of fish. We would have clam cakes, clams on the half shell, clam chowder, etc, etc. Other times it would be lobsters or crabs. If he couldn't sleep, he would have pizza made for the midnight shift change. We were soooo spoiled. During WWII, US Army's Sgt. Ray was a cook in General Eisenhower's kitchen. Ike loved mayonnaise and couldn't get it shipped over to him. Ray knew how to make it from scratch.

My wife Marion, aside from being smart, gorgeous, a great mother and fun, was also adventuresome. Tom Sullivan owned 80 acres of woods upstate New York near Hudson and during the season, we would go deer hunting. Sleeping in an old farmhouse with no heat upstairs, just 100 lbs. of blankets and getting up at 5:00AM and then going out to the snow covered ground did not stop Marion. She even volunteered to be part of a sweep through the woods to drive the deer towards shooters and that did not deter her. I wish for all that effort we actually got a deer.

Marion and I started living pretty good with my new position. We bought a fence for our back yard and put in a fancy 24' in diameter, above ground swimming pool. My Mom loved to play with the kids in pool during summer visits. We always were with Jack and Carol's clan as well. Our kids, with their cousins, played together from the earliest ages which developed a closeness that would last their entire lives. Our house was so nice that Marion's parents would "vacation" in Smithtown. That was great company for Marion when I was out "playing with my boat" in New York harbor. We went through a couple of dogs but settled on Greta, a beautiful German Short haired Pointer. She was a great family dog.

Marion's first husband Paul had a sister Carol. She was older than my brother but regardless we all grew up in the same apartment house on Gelston Avenue. Don and I were actually the altar boys when Carol married John Jacobs. When Marion and I moved to Smithtown, we became closer to the Jacobs, hiring their older girls, especially Donna, as babysitters. The Jacobs lived close to us in Commack, NY, about a 15 minute drive. We enjoyed each others company and did a number of things together, like buying a small one design sailboat, a Penguin, which I raced locally. We spent Thanksgiving's together for several years.

It came to pass that one week, I was asked not to join the Massachusetts, but instead report to the Esso Pelham at Bayway, NJ. The Pelham was an integrated tug/barge unit and relatively small. Her purpose was to resupply distributors in often remote parts of the New York harbor area. The Esso Pelham was a 1400 HP, twin screw tug with "flanking rudders." The four additional rudders, two to a propeller, were in front of each propeller. This allowed the tug to be steered going astern as well as going ahead. This was a revolutionary idea at the time with the steering wheel replaced by levers, one for the main rudders and the other for the flankers. The barge, the Esso Tow No.1, carried 10,000 barrels of assorted clean petroleum products. She was considered to be a "drugstore" tank vessel often carrying 3 grades of gasoline, kerosene and home heating fuel on one trip.

I was actually riding as a mate to be taught by Captain Paul Lewis, not only to operate the tug, to load and discharge the barge, but also how to get in and out of some of the tightest little creeks around New York. The deckhands were great in performing their duties handling lines as well as loading and discharging the Tow 1, but before that week was over, I knew that barge like the back of my hand. I even found a valve on deck that none of the regulars knew what that valve did. It turned out to be a pumping system crossover valve, up forward, that no one ever used.

We received orders to load for a trip to our namesake, Pelham, NY. The terminal was all the way up to the head of the Hutchinson River in the Bronx. It was a creek that you went into on half tide rising, discharged your cargo and left on half tide falling. Any delay would result in being stuck in there waiting for the next tide. The entrance to the creek was the most treacherous with a rock ledge channel with 120 degree turns and 2 bridges offset from each other. We got to the entrance when Capt. Paul almost passed out and said to me: "Russ, you've got it." I had no choice but to proceed and my knees started shaking. You couldn't attempt those bridges at dead slow ahead since you needed to get up to steerage speed. My knees were knocking and did not stop until we were alongside the berth. Come to find out, Paul was a Korean War veteran and suffered what we later know as PTSD. It was a good thing I was there and up in the wheelhouse learning. I learned in a hurry. I later became the vacation relief man for the two Captains on the Pelham and as such learned all about practically every little hole in the wall in and around New York: Eastchester Creek, Newtown Creek, Gowanus Canal, Roundout Creek in Kingston, NY, the water route to Idewild Airport, the Raritan River, the Passaic River and I became an expert running the Hackensack River. When I can't sleep, instead of counting sheep, I usually pilot the Pelham up the Hackensack in my mind.

I vividly remember every buoy and every bridge in that waterway to this day. Just before getting to the Esso Terminal in the Hackensack, there was a drive in movie with its giant outdoor screen. Once they were playing "Rosemary's Baby" and the scene where Rosemary was being disrobed for the Devil, coincided with me passing by on the Pelham. I came close to putting the Tow 1 into the reeds before I recovered.

MT Esso Massachusetts

MT Esso Pelham

CHAPTER 24

My brother-in-law Steve Carbone, married to Evelyn, had been employed as a teacher at Bishop Loughlin high school in Brooklyn. By 1967, they had two children, Mathew and Michelle. Steve applied for and was accepted on July 24th, 1967 to train to be a Special Agent in the Federal Bureau of Investigation, the FBI, WOW! He went off to Quantico, Virginia in August to begin that training. What a great move. After multiple weeks of training, he and Evelyn packed up the kids and their household and went to Columbia, NC for his first assignment. How exciting.

It happened that in 1968, Local 333 went out on strike for a long time, 64 days, for a reason I cannot remember. The major oil companies had to feel vindicated for having their own fleets of equipment because there were no interruptions of their supply. We had an additional benefit of no loss of income. The oil companies agreed that what ever the union employees got as additional wages, they would match it with us, retroactively. The strike ended and we got our retroactive pay as a separate check. Marion and I decided that we should use that bonus to actually go on a honeymoon. We were so lucky to have the Jacob's living close by who agreed to watch Scott while Marion's parents had Paul.

My suggestion was, speaking from the experience of actually having been there, was to go to Puerto Rico. Due to my Moran/Barge Caribbean experience, I suggested the San Juan Hyatt, the tallest hotel on Condado Beach. I told the travel agent that I wanted a room on the 15th floor or above with a westward exposure. I knew that would overlook Morro Castle and the harbor entrance so we could see ship traffic into and out of San Juan harbor. It would also avail us of the beautiful sunsets of Puerto Rico while enjoying our evening cocktail. .This was Marion's first experience that included air travel and the flight down on Eastern Airlines was excellent. We decided mid-week that an air hop to St. Thomas would be fun. It was a small prop plane and all went well with our flight and the visit to a neighboring island. On the return flight the pilot left the door open to the cockpit so we could hear all the radio traffic for the return flight to San Juan. As we approached San Juan Airport, we could hear our pilot's conversation with the control tower: "We've got a 727 coming in, but if you think you can beat him in, go ahead." We knew what dive bomber pilots must have felt during WWII, left wing up and dive for the end of the runway! We had touchdown on the landing strip and as we turned off the main strip to a side road, we felt the WHOOSH of the 727 going by our tail. Marion wasn't happy about flying.

The next day we were leaving our island paradise to go home. Boarding went easily and before we knew it our Eastern Airliner was airborne. I noticed a strange vibration in the plane after take off and sure enough, it wasn't long before the Captain announced that there was a malfunction not allowing him to get the wheels retracted. "We are going to go out over the ocean to dump some fuel and then return to San Juan." After 40 minutes of making small circles, we lined up to land. The wheels touched down, the brakes squealed, the reverse thrusters screamed at full power and the plane finally stopped at the end of the runway with the front wheels in the dirt. Marion, on her first fly away vacation was about to melt in her seat. "Is there a ship available to take us home?"

When I got out of the door of the plane I ran to the Pan Am desk to try to get two seats to New York and I did. I'm glad I ran, since there were very few seats available. This was a smooth flight and we safely returned to New York. Driving up to the Jacob's house where Scott had been, there was Scott in his highchair out on the front lawn. Turns out they agreed that Scott was not the easiest child to watch.

During the summer of 1967, there was a warming trend in the Northern Hemisphere that made less ice north of Canada. Esso purchased a tank vessel of 100,000 tons capacity and altered it with an ice breaking bow and stainless steel propellers to make a voyage across the Northern Passage. It was named the Esso Manhattan. Its' voyage from the Alaskan oil fields to the Esso refinery in Elizabeth, NJ was a complete success. To celebrate, Esso decided to dock the Manhattan at the passenger ship terminal on Manhattan's West side and invite the press and guests to see her. My tug, the Esso Massachusetts, was designated the Press Boat and I got to ferry around some of the news hosts we watch on TV every night. It was a fun day for my crew and I. Unfortunately, the next year saw the northern ice sock in solid, precluding temporarily any more Northern Passage voyages. On and off global warming and cooling seemed a bit unpredictable depending on the Sun.

Standard Oil Company
INCORPORATED IN New Jersey

30 ROCKEFELLER PLAZA, NEW YORK, N.Y. 10020   Public Relations Department

November 20, 1969

Captain Russell McVay
Marine Department
Humble Oil & Refining Company
Post Office Bin C
Bayonne, New Jersey 07002

Dear Russ:

On behalf of Jersey Standard and all the reporters and cameramen aboard the Esso Manhattan on November 12, I'd like to thank you very much for the great job you and your crew did in escorting us around the harbor.

I'd never been aboard a tug, and enjoyed the ride. But many of the press guys had been on tugs several times in the past and they told me they had never received such friendly cooperation from any tugboat skipper.

You and your crew played a very important part in obtaining the wide coverage accorded the arrival of the S.S. Manhattan. Again, many thanks and best regards.

Sincerely,

Jack Murphy

JFM:eah

cc: Mr. A. Giallorenzi

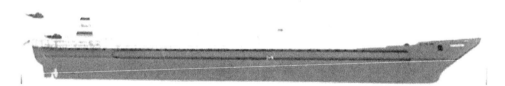

Steve and Evelyn's assignment in Columbia, NC was followed by his next assignment to the Detroit, MI, FBI office. My week on, week off schedule made a visit to Detroit feasible. We had bought an Oldsmobile Vista Cruiser station wagon, so we had a nice big vehicle to pack up the kids and our gear for a week on the road. The weather was beautiful as we drove to our first stop of Niagara Falls, NY. We stayed overnight and took in the whole scene. The sheer power and roar made Niagara Falls was as good as the reviews about it. We crossed into Canada and got on the Queen Elizabeth highway that took us directly to Detroit. Evelyn and Steve had bought a house in the St. Claire Shores neighborhood near the Welland Canal connecting Lake Huron and Lake

Erie. We had a thoroughly good time with this visit. Our return trip brought us through Pennsylvania and we stayed overnight in East Stroudsberg, on the Delaware Water Gap between Pennsylvania and New Jersey. That was on a Monday night. The next day at Noon, Tuesday, was crew change day, so Marion dropped me off at Pier 6 Staten Island to join the Massachusetts and then went home from there. What a great week.

We worked 12 hours daily, two 6 hour shifts with mine, as Captain, from 0600 to noon and then 1800 to midnight. That was another perk of being Captain, having working hours close to normal living, leaving no big adjustment when you got home. The Mate's midnight to 0600 watch was a killer to do for a whole week aboard, causing a lot of yawning when you were home. There was an interesting summer when the Massachusetts was assigned to bring 25,00 bbl barge loads of heavy oil from Bayway, NJ to South Hartford, CT, up the Connecticut River. On the first trip, I was assigned a new Mate who was a docking pilot in the Esso facility over in Saudi Arabia. He was a seasoned sailor but had no knowledge of Long Island Sound. On that first trip, I was awakened at 0200 one morning and when I went to the pilot house, the fog was so thick you could not see the bow of the barge we were towing alongside. Long Island Sound was like my back yard and with one glance at the radar, I could see that we were off New Haven. I got us safely anchored inside the breakwater and we waited it out for clear sailing. For that first trip up the Connecticut River, I took a local Pilot. He said he had made a call to an old timer in Middletown, CT who had a photo collection of every vessel that transited the Connecticut River since the 1930's. The old timer got very excited when he found out that a Captain McVay was in charge on the Esso Massachusetts because I wasn't the first and that we were distant cousins. Grandpa would have been proud. After two trips, no local pilot was necessary.

CHAPTER 25

Towards the end of 1969, I was getting the feeling that I had assisted docking ships at every terminal in New York harbor and that I had towed or assisted on every oil barge operating in my area. I did get another honor working at Esso.

The Company built 2 brand new tugs for the New York operation, The Esso Garden State and the Esso Empire State. They gave me the Captain's job of the Empire State. It was just a larger version of the Esso Pelham with flanking rudders, so it was very comfortable for me. They were totally automated though, not requiring an engineer. We could start and stop the main engines, two Caterpillar diesels and stop and switch generators from the pilothouse. The toilets were a new electric type that had their drawbacks. I was asked to demonstrate a typical job of moving a barge from A to B for the Esso Marine Department officials from Houston. While picking up one of the barges at Constable Hook, NJ, one of the guests used the electric head. Flushing meant incinerating what you put into the toilet, the result of the incineration was discharged from a short stack above the pilothouse. Getting bathed in boiled urine did not go over too well with our dignitaries, those who designed this vessel. The toilets were replaced quickly. The designed crew was a Captain and Mate plus 2 deckhands. No engineer and no cook.

The no engineer part lasted until one of the new boats had an overspeed governor failure on one of the main engines that resulted in a completely blown engine. They started carrying one engineer after that incident.

In the middle of having to make these critical decisions, my five year anniversary of graduating from Kings Point came upon us. It was a fun event to mingle with fellow graduates of the Class of '64 and try to get caught up among friends. Marion wore a gold covered dress and had her hair professionally done. She was more than beautiful to the point some classmates commented "McVay married a movie star." No movies but certainly a star in my mind.

If a Docking Pilot's position was about to open up at Esso, I certainly would have been in line to be awarded that spot, but those positions were full with fairly young people. Realistically, a Pilot's spot would not be available for another 10 years. It was not that I was bored with my lot in life; I was just ready to try something else and there was the good thought of being home every night. There was no opportunity to be had at Esso's Marine Department in Houston, Texas. I got the feeling that as a tugboat man, I would be swallowed up by the big ship mentality that was present there.

My additional experience observing what transpired in all of New York harbor, it was evident to me that if I was going to try to get a shore job in a tugboat company, I ought to do it with "the best in the business," Moran. Not only that, I was thoroughly familiar with every piece of Moran's equipment in New York as well as interacting with their equipment in the Middle Atlantic states.

Marion and I both agreed what the first step might be, was to seek the council of Bob Wilson, Marion's old boss, who was now the Manager of Sales for Curtis Bay Towing. His office was still part of the Moran office at 17 Battery Place where they had the whole 25th floor. Here is some history that I came to know over time. The Moran family had several factions at that time, involved in Moran Towing Corp. and subsidiaries. Admiral Edmond J. Moran was clearly the most powerful of the family leaders and was Chairman of the Board. His reputation for his leadership in the Normandy Invasion in WWII preceded him wherever he went. He was however getting on in years, so he tapped his oldest son Thomas E. Moran to be his successor, assuming the role of President. Thomas was a Vice President of Marine Transport Lines when his father called. Another faction was lead by Mr. Frank Belford whose mother was Agnes Moran, 1st cousin to the Admiral and being older than Thomas, thought he was in line to succeed the Admiral. Frank Belford was President of Seaboard Shipping Corp., the oil transportation subsidiary of Moran. Seaboard was quite a large company servicing customers in the New York State barge Canal and into the Great Lakes. They also serviced local customers, like Shell Oil Company's ship bunkering business, all with their large fleet of barges.

My resume was written with Bob Wilson's assistance and was submitted first to his friend, Lloyd Graham, Moran's Vice President of Sales. Bob Wilson was enthusiastic, presenting my case saying "here is a 27 year old man, licensed Captain and First Class Pilot for all of the New York area, with five years experience as a tug and tanker Captain and a graduate of the U.S. Merchant Marine Academy at Kings Point." Lloyd Graham circulated it to everyone in the upper management of Moran. Bob Wilson heard that clearly they wanted to hire me but they did not know where to put me. Finally, both Mr. Graham and Mr. Belford said I was hired.

It was sad leaving my crew and friends from Esso after spending so much time with them over the years. When Captain Krieger heard where I was going, he said it was inevitable. He always introduced me to his associates "as the greatest thing since the invention of the compass." Even Chuck Sheelan, the personnel manager, was sad to see me go, so I knew I would get good references.

My first assignment was vague, working for both the Moran sales department under Mr. Graham and also for Seaboard Shipping Co. under Mr. Belford. I vividly remember being invited to have lunch with Mr. Belford and his Vice President at the Downtown Athletic Club in the building next door to 17 Battery Place. The DAC was the preferred lunch spot for most of the Maritime and Insurance company's executives. The 3rd floor sported the longest bar in Manhattan at 80 feet long. We went to the more sedate restaurant on the 12th floor. After the usual pleasantries, the killer question was asked. "As a Captain towing all these barges around, how does the Seaboard equipment stack up to the other barge company's equipment?" I said that it was obvious that Seaboard's equipment was older, but it seemed to be well maintained. "From a tug boatman's point of view, the extra time it takes to tie up a Seaboard barge, is a pain in the neck, especially in the winter. All of your barges are equipped with manila rope tie up lines. In the winter those lines freeze and become unmanageable, they are so stiff. It can take sometimes almost an hour to tie up at a berth. As in most things, time is money. All of the other barges in the port use Dacron composites which are so much stronger and easier to use." I did not know if I put my foot in it, but I figured it was best to be honest.

It just happened once that I was in the Dispatchers office when Admiral Moran came in as well. He looked out the window and saw the Diana Moran towing the B-110 passing around the Battery (Lower Manhattan). "What is my beautiful tug doing towing that filthy looking barge?" Despite the fact that he was correct in his description of Bouchard's oldest looking barge (a rarity for Bouchard), I gathered he was not a fan of oil barges. And here I am a salesman for "those filthy looking things."

Having me as a salesman was kind of a waste, in my opinion. It didn't last long because "Mr. Moran," Thomas that is, decided that he wanted to bring all of Moran's operations under the same insurance Club, tugs and barges. He also wanted all outstanding insurance claims for the barges to be settled prior to the merging and that was a big project. "Give it to the new guy, see what he can do."

As dull and droll as that may sound, settling insurance claims, proved to be a very educational experience. The relationship of doing the work with tugs and barges to what it costs and what accidents meant in lost time and revenue was a terrific education. I also had the pleasure of working closely with Mr. Joseph Meseck, Moran's Insurance Manager. When Moran acquired Meseck Towing Co., they not only got some very fine tugs, they fortunately also got Joe, a really smart and really nice man. Aside from the financial aspects of examining mistakes leading to damages, I got exposed to all the types of work in which Seaboard Shipping was involved and the shipyards where they had most repairs done. That gave me insight into the tactics shipyards used in preparing bills. On occasion where I had to read the Damage Reports submitted by crew members who were there, both tug crews and tankermen, my real life experience doing that work sometimes allowed me to spot a BS story by someone wanting to place blame on the other. Bouchard Transportation was famous for this. It was said that the first thing Bouchard taught its new tankermen was how to fill out a damage report. The tugs are always at fault.

A funny thing happened shortly after starting in the office at Moran. One day, Terry O'Conner, the office manager, showed up at my desk with two others and happily awarded me my five year pin. Their records didn't show that I left Moran to go to Esso for three years.

That particular Seaboard project ended after a few weeks satisfactorily only to have another follow, but in a different direction. Seaboard had contracted with Todd Shipyard Corp. to build a barge that had to comply with the following:

1. It was to be the largest barge that could fit in the locks of New York's Erie Barge Canal
2. It had propellers aft, powered off the back end of the pump engines that were used to move the barge out of one lock and then wait for the tug to come up on a second locking. It was basically self propelled.
3. The propellers could also be steered from a remote in the tug's pilothouse. This would help boost the unit's speed.
4. The tanks would be coated with something new called epoxy, to accommodate the carriage of chemical products.

The name of the barge was to be the Chemical #1 and it did not turn out to be such a good idea.

The barge and its sophisticated equipment, suffered many delays and breakdowns, many of which were shipyard related in the original construction. Problems for customers and their claims with Seaboard and ultimately against Todd Shipyard mounted weekly. This all happened prior to my tenure of working in the office but now Seaboard/Moran had to do something about it. Tom Moran took over. He called me into his office one day and explained the problem and that he had taken over what was going to be the negotiation with Todd Shipyard. He wanted me to be thorough in my examination into the faults and the results in monetary losses. I developed a method to track the problems and what they cost us in a visual display that could be easily understood. I used a simple 13 column pad listing a short explanation of the incident, the time lost and the cost. When a page was full, I taped another below it creating a chronicle. (Authors note: this was 1970)

When I was done, the study was 15 pages making it 15 feet long which I rolled up like a scroll.

One day when I was working on the Chem 1 project, Mr. Moran came to me and invited me to join him at a luncheon. It was a Maritime Association affair that would have all the local steamship company executives as well all the major tugboat company executives. It was held at the Whitehall Club, just a short walk next door to our building. The first person I was introduced to by Mr. Moran was J.P. MacAllister, head of Moran's biggest competitor, MacAllister Brothers Towing Corp..... "JP, meet my Kings Pointer, Captain Russ McVay."

Mr. MacAllister asked me if I was any relation to Captain Harold McVay and when I said he was my father, he gave me a big hug. "If you are half the man your father was, you'll be great." I had no idea where that came from, which I passed on to Mr. Moran.

Getting hugged by the chief competitor couldn't be good. Mr. Moran continued introducing me around as his "Kings Pointer."

As soon as we were back at the office, I called my Mom and related what had just happened. It was the first time that I heard the story of JP giving my parents money and them paying it back. I was happy to pass that story on to Mr. Moran.

When the appointment time came, just Mr. Moran and myself went to Todd Shipyard's corporate office. We met with Mr.

Arthur Stout, President of Todd and a small cadre of his assistants in their gigantic board room overlooking New York harbor. The total damages that I had calculated the claim to be was right around $200,000 in repairs and lost time. I had memorized all the details of each claim, in case they wanted to dissect it piece by piece. Instead Mr. Stout was very cavalier in his speech and made a quick offer to settle this nuisance for $50,000: "after all how did you possibly keep track of all this?"

"Roll out your Dead Sea Scroll Russ." It was a pet name Mr. Moran used referring to my work. Needless to say, seeing 15 feet of papers containing details of each and every item, they were taken by surprise. It added a whole new attitude to this negotiation and Mr. Moran managed to settle for $150,000. He was elated and I got a "good job" from the boss.

Back on the home front, Marion and I were enjoying my new schedule of being home every night and every weekend. We were also happy to share the good news that Marion was pregnant once again with a due date in November. It would still be alright in our house where Paul and Scott could now share the bunk bed we had in one room and the other room being available for a baby's room. During these times we continued to have fun times with Jack and Carol plus kids. There was also a newcomer to our home.

Marion's youngest sister Geraldine was seriously dating a fellow Brooklynite, Dennis Gallagher. Dennis had worked for Merritt Chapman and Scott, a huge maritime corporation specializing in salvage operations and heavy lift marine applications. Dennis actually worked aboard one of their large salvage tugs, the "Curb," so we had a lot to talk about. Dennis was a good guy and having he and Geraldine joining us was very welcome.

With all this drama going on at work at this time, it did not match what was going on at home.

Edith and Joe were stationed in Seattle, Washington and she was pregnant and due to deliver in March. The ship that Joe was an officer aboard was at sea near Hawaii doing NOAA projects. Edith already had her two sons Christopher and Andrew with her, so she had her hands full. My Mom flew out to Seattle to help over Christmas vacation but had to return to her job as a teacher in St. Patrick's School. On March 7th, Edith gave birth to not one, but two beautiful babies, one boy and one girl, at the U.S. Navy hospital in Seattle. It is hard to believe even in those days that having twins was not diagnosed, yet it was a surprise. Edith's physical condition was not good. Tragedy struck! Edith succumbed to a bout with toxemia. Joe, upon arrival back home, must have been stunned to find himself now a father of four children and no wife.

Don and I went to Brooklyn with heavy hearts and the sad duty to tell Mom about Edith. We both went to the Principle's office and as graduates of St. Pat's ourselves, we knew where to go. She was called out of her class and as soon as she spotted us, she knew......it was a heart wrenching experience for us all, her losing a child and us a sibling. That was an experience I would never want to have to repeat.

Marion and I and Don and Cathy knew we had to help. Cathy volunteered to go to Seattle and to take the twins home and when she got back we would each take one to care for until their future was decided. We got the girl baby, by then named Donna, while Don and Cathy kept Danny. In spite of her already being pregnant, Marion always loved having a baby to care for and we already had a room set up for a baby.

Joe's life was certainly in turmoil and he finally had to put his career on hold until he could settle the issues with his kids. Joe's Mom stepped up and offered to take Chris and Andy to her house in the upstate town of Walton, New York. My Mom kept warning Marion that as soon as Joe and his Mom decided to reunite all four kids, she better be prepared to do it sooner rather than later. The longer Marion had Donna, the harder it was going to be to let her go. In fact Marion and I offered to take her permanently, an offer that was never addressed. Eventually, that summer, Joe and his Mom decided that they wanted to get all four kids together. Marion was heart broken but we of course would comply. My Mom came with us on that long trip from Long Island to Walton, NY to Grandma Dropp's house. We stopped enroute, in the Catskill Mountains, to have lunch at a roadside diner. Marion had Donna in her arms and of course she was already five months pregnant when a rude woman chided Marion as a pig for having another baby with another in her arms. My mother overheard that and went after that woman verbally, yelling about delivering my dead daughter's child to her father after taking care of his child.......you have some nerve......until the woman had to leave. This just added to the morose feelings we all suffered.

Meanwhile, back at Moran, my job was still not really defined and I was getting frustrated. I was frustrated enough to call Chuck Sheelan at Esso to inquire as to whether a spot would be available at my old job, if I left Moran. He assured me that there would be, just say when. Marion and I discussed it at length and we decided that I should resign from Moran. On that fateful day, she told me to just let her know what train I'd be on and she would come and get me. It was a day I will never forget. Upon arrival at the office, I asked Jim Sheeran, the Assistant Manager of Seaboard Shipping, if we could speak in private. I discussed my mounting frustration over having a still undefined purpose at Moran and that since Esso would welcome me back, I am feeling I should resign. He tried to talk me out of it, but in the end he conceded that if that is what I wanted, then do it. Walking down the hall toward Mr. Moran's office, I encountered him heading for his office. "Sir, I'd like to speak to you if you have time." "Oh good Russ, I want to talk to you myself." So we went into his office and sat down. "OK Russ, what do want?" "No sir, you go first."

"OK! I was thinking we should explore whether there is any business that we could develop in the oil transportation trade down in the Chesapeake Bay area and the only way we'll know is to give it a try. So, I want to form a new Company, separate from Moran, and send you down there to see what you can generate. I thought we'll give you two tugs and two barges to get started. You'll move to Norfolk, you'll be the President of this Company and you can make your wife Vice President and you'll run it from your house………...a family company. Does that sound good to you?" "Yes SIR!" "Now, what did you want Russ?"

"NOTHING."

CHAPTER 26

Could anything else be thrown into 1970?? Let's see: a change of job and Companies, going from working afloat to a shore side job with a daily commute, the tragic loss of Edith and the helping with the kids and now selling our house and moving to Norfolk, VA. Also, we could not forget that all this time, Marion was pregnant.

Evelyn and Steve were living in Alexandria, Virginia where Steve was attending an FBI school for an intense education course learning to speak and understand the Chinese language. He was to be transferred to the New York city office of the FBI. They made several trips to the Long Island area, house hunting, using our house as a home base. When it became clear that we were being transferred to Norfolk and were going sell our house, Steve said, "Why don't we buy your house." We searched the real estate market to get comparable sales of our size house in the neighborhood and discovered that $32,000 seemed to be the fair price. Steve and Evelyn agreed. It happened that a childhood friend of Marion's had moved into our neighborhood, Sue Brennan, now Sue Trueber and she was married to a lawyer, Bill

Trueber. He drew up all the documents needed to complete this transaction. It could not get any easier for both of us.

Since we were not sure if Norfolk was going to be the right spot to obtain business for my little fleet, we decided that we should find an apartment to live in initially. Just south of Little Creek in Virginia Beach, we found a new apartment complex being built with completed units available. It had a very nice grade school within walking distance of where Paul, at age seven, would go into the second grade. Scott was only four and too young for school. Our apartment was big with three bedrooms and two baths, plenty of room for us, the two kids and one on the way.

Quite frankly, I do not know how we did it all. Aside from all the moving details, which Marion handled completely, she also had to find a new OBGYN to take over for an eight month pregnancy, set up a pediatrician for Scott, locate the hospitals in case of emergency………etc, etc. She also had to get Paul enrolled in school.

There was a couple of weeks delay before the first tug/barge unit would arrive, giving me a chance to get organized. Mr. Moran set up a meeting for me to meet Capt. Frank Hughes, President and Dick Tillman, VP Finance of Moran's subsidiary Curtis Bay Towing Co. Their corporate headquarters for the three ports they operate in was Baltimore, MD. Capt. Hughes was very helpful and remembered Marion from her working in their New York sales office. With their help I completed corporate registration and name changes in Wilmington, Delaware, where many of Moran/Curtis Bay tugs were home ported. Mr. Tillman was also very helpful in getting me set up with bank accounts and accounting people to help me with the book keeping responsibilities of our little company.

While I was in Baltimore, I took the opportunity to visit the large Esso terminal located in Baltimore harbor and was fortunate enough to meet the head of operations, Bob Williams. That terminal took in shiploads of petroleum products and distributed them via truck and also barges. Bob was intrigued with my operation and because I was a former Esso tug employee, he promised to give our BarTran Inc. tug and barge a try. It was there that I got the feeling that there was a need for another small barge operator in the Northern Chesapeake and the Delaware river.

This whole operation was going to run from a small desk in our bedroom. I wasn't quite sure where I was going to get a competent crew to man the tug and especially certified tankermen for the barge, so I ran an ad in the Norfolk newspaper. "Crewmembers to man a tugboat and oil barge unit that will be operating in the Chesapeake Bay. All proper licenses, tankerman certifications and seaman's cards required." The same day that the newspaper came out, I got a call from Parksley, VA…... "Hi this is Capt. Bill from Parksley and I can run that boat for you." We agreed to meet half way since Parksley was quite a distance up the Delmarva Peninsula. We met and sure enough he had a 300 ton Master's license and some First Class Pilotage for Chesapeake Bay. He was very happy with my offer for his pay of $140/day and when I asked him if he knew any others who could fill the other billets, especially certified tankermen, he answered: "Tell me the total daily payroll number you'll pay." I told him $585/day for a crew consisting of 1-Captain,1 mate, one engineer (Licensed), 2 deckhands and a cook. The tankerman would be separate at $110 per day and the tug deckhands would help him. He asked for a deal to give him that money and he would fill all positions with good competent people. I told him I would agree, if he would assemble them all for me to interview.

Interview was the wrong word because these men were all from Tangier Island, a small island in the Chesapeake whose people are unique in life style and language. The assembled crew were all boatmen, being brought up on the waters of the Bay. Their language was strange, British, with a strong twist of a southern accent on American English made conversing difficult, but they were all properly documented and pleasant. I made it very clear that the first sign of anyone drinking alcoholic beverages while aboard, the entire crew would lose their jobs. I would go elsewhere to man the units.

Now it was time to take possession of our first tug/barge unit. The barge was Seaboard Shipping's barge Panhandle, a 24,000 barrel capacity black oil barge renamed the BarTran #1. The tug was the Margot Moran, a 1200 HP, single screw tug. They were delivered to me in a small shipyard in Wilmington, Del. Where I had them repainted to our new colors including the new name for the Margot, the tug "Marion." It was the least I could do for this magnificent woman who worked right alongside me to accomplish this job.

When we were ready to go, Bob Williams at Esso gave me our first job: a full load of #6 fuel oil delivered to the Delmarva Power & Light generating station in Seaford, DE and loaded at Esso's Baltimore terminal. The barge Bartran No.1 was ideally suited for this trade because, she carried a full load at a shallow draft.

I wanted to make this job go as smooth as can be, so I joined the crew for the entire trip in my work clothes and gloves. I am glad I did as far as the tankerman was concerned, since I was able to assist loading and discharging based on my previous experience on the Tow #1 at Esso. It was also a perfect opportunity to assess the crew. There was no problem with the pilothouse crew on the tug. They were obviously seasoned boat handlers, even going up to the head of the winding and shallow Wicomico River to Seaford, DE. I helped with the steering, making up the tow and discharging the barge, something that was fun for me. It was important to me also, that these men knew that I knew as much or more than they did and was not just an office suit. That successful first voyage led to more with Esso.

Encouraged, I wound up making sales calls on all the refineries in Delaware, Philadelphia and New Jersey located on the Delaware River, drumming up business right away from the Gulf Oil refinery in South Philadelphia. There were also good prospects from the Texaco Refinery as well as the Refineries of Sunoco, Esso and Mobil Oil. We all became experts at navigating the Chesapeake and Delaware Canal. Between Esso and Gulf Oil, the barge BarTran#1 was kept busy for the rest of the year.

It was obvious after some time that the Norfolk, Hampton Roads areas was not the place for this fledgling company office to be located. This one man show had me spending too much time on the road and out of contact. (Author's note: no cell phones then). Marion was answering phones and getting messages to me as quickly as possible. This was on top of helping Paul with school work, caring for Scott and attending doctor's appointments pre-delivery of child #3. Marion met a young girl in our complex of about age 15, Barbara Wheatley, who became our permanent baby sitter and a life long friend. What a delight to have her around, she was so pleasant and Paul and Scott took to her immediately.

Marion was due to give birth in early November and sure enough on November 5, 1970 we now had another boy, a beautiful baby born in Virginia Beach hospital. He was to be named Michael Gerard McVay, reversed name of Gerard Michael, Marion's Dad. Marion's preference was that he'll be called Mike or Michael and I agreed.

After Michael was born we really wanted to move to Maryland to get closer to the actual work being done with our tug/barge unit. The search was on and we loved it. We always managed to look at houses that were slightly more expensive than we could afford. I always felt we would "grow" into them having confidence that my salary would continue to rise.

We zeroed in on one beautiful house in Crofton, MD but at $44,700, the monthly payment was just a little bit more than the bank would approve for a mortgage. We were so disappointed. About a week later, our saleswoman, who was helping us, said that the interest rate just dropped enough to make the monthly payment within our reach. WE'LL TAKE IT!! It was a beautiful house on a quiet street for the kids.

So, now along with building a start up business and not a simple business at that, we add to that a newborn and moving to a new home and in a different State. Thank God for the energy of youth. Crofton was a wonderful community to join. It had a Country Club, golf course, clubhouse, etc, if you chose to join, it was not mandatory. It was also a bedroom community for many who were employed by the government in Washington, DC, though not all, as our next door neighbor was an airline pilot for Eastern Airlines. Most importantly it was a young community with lots of kids and good schools. Paul got interested in Little League which helped us parents meet up with similar aged groups.

After game activities let us get introduced to local restaurants like Buzzy's in Annapolis. It was there that we were to discover the pleasure of eating blue claw crabs, something we still enjoy today. Buzzy's had picnic tables covered with brown paper, wooden mallets for cracking crabs and plenty of Old Bay Seasoning. There was also a live Honky Tonk band playing on a small stage in the back.

Paul's friends in Crofton also loved fishing and fished every pond in Crofton's golf course. I wound up initiating occasional trips with five or six neighborhood kids to ocean fishing out of Ocean City, MD. At midnight of the appointed day, I would pile the kids in our car and they would sleep for the entire 4 ½ hour trip to the ocean. The fishing boat would leave the dock at 5:30AM and return about 2:00PM and our group would have heavy bags of seabass and porgies that we caught. I would also have a pile of kids fast asleep for the whole drive home.

In Crofton, you could never say: "Gee, there's nothing to do this weekend." Washington was 35 minutes away; downtown Baltimore was 30 minutes away and Annapolis was 15 minutes away, all terrific tourist attractions. In one of our excursions to the Naval Academy, we went to the sailing center and in their trophy room, we found a plaque for the first Shield's Class interAcademy race that was won by: Graham Hall, Russell McVay and Robert Lindmark of USMMA.

In spite of all this activity, we managed to find time to buy a dog, a German Shepherd pup named Sheila. Geraldine and Dennis loved coming to Maryland so much that they were there almost every weekend. Living in Crofton was a great experience.

The BarTran equipment stayed busy that whole Fall and Winter's beginning. The second unit was now scheduled to arrive in Baltimore in January and it was the sister barge to the BarTran #1 and the tug was similar to the Marion. That tug was renamed the "Capt. Harold," after my Dad and of course the barge was named BarTran #2. Our success spurred conversations with Bob Williams at Esso suggesting that he could keep a 25,000 bbl clean oil barge busy for most of the year. That would mean new construction since Moran had no unit like that to put into service.

I had to get help and luckily a fellow responded to my advertising for a crew for the second unit. Bobbie Hague was a certified tankerman and had served in the engine room of an assortment of tugboats. I could not have asked for a better Port Engineer for me, one who could relieve just some of the 24/7 requirements of running this small Company.

CHAPTER 27

In the Spring of 1971, Dennis and Geraldine tied the knot. We traveled from Crofton to Brooklyn for the beautiful wedding in St. Anselm's Catholic Church. Marion was in the wedding party as Matron of Honor opposite Dennis' brother John who was Best Man. The reception was held at the beautiful Hamilton House near the shore in Bay Ridge Brooklyn. A great time was had by all.

The vessels that I was operating in the Chesapeake Bay and Delaware River were manned with non union crews, after being transferred out of Local 333 jurisdiction in New York. Local 333 demanded that their jurisdiction was wherever Moran Towing went on the planet. Over the months they exerted more and more pressure on Moran, insisting that even though those tugs and barges never came near New York, that they should be manning them. I was never really made privy to the actual fights that must have taken place, but the net effect was that I was shut down. My fleet was repainted and sent back to New York. Over those same months, BarTran Corp. was actually making decent profits, so it was worth exploring different ways to possibly keep that idea alive. A meeting was to be held in Captain Hughes' office with myself and Dick Tillman. On the telephone was Tom Moran, Marty Carroll, Vice President of Moran and Lee Christensen, Vice President, Finance and Accounting.

It was told to me that fighting Local 333 about manning vessels that they had a history of manning could present very costly battles both operationally and legally. We explored continuing the Chesapeake Bay oil barge operation using equipment that had never had Local 333 crews assigned to those vessels. Also, Curtis Bay Towing's tugs were all manned by Union crews from the Seafarer's International Union (SIU). It was agreed that Marty Carroll, Captain Hughes and myself would meet with the SIU to discuss or negotiate a contract that would cover the barge operation. What a difference dealing with the SIU over 333. The New York union was just confrontational on every item discussed. The SIU wanted to do whatever would make the barge company successful and they would be happy to get more employees under their wing. I felt the crew members would also be happier to pick up the benefits of health insurance and pensions offered by the union. The next question addressed was what equipment was available. It happened that Seaboard Shipping already had a barge under construction that was going to used in the New York State barge canal trade. Profit margins in that trade were not the greatest, compared to the Chesapeake operation so, the Barge New Jersey was going to be assigned to me. She was a 36,000 bbl, heavy oil designed barge that I knew I could keep busy with Gulf Oil Co. alone. With this larger barge in the picture, Hess Oil Company became another player with work for our new company. Hess had a large terminal in the Curtis Bay section of Baltimore harbor. While exploring other options, I mentioned that Bob Williams from Esso said that he could keep a clean oil barge busy all year if one were available. I was tasked to explore that option which would involve new construction. My first task was to examine what trade Esso planned to use a clean oil barge, so I met with Bob Williams several times so we could provide a barge that was suitable to his needs. He was looking for a barge capable of carrying "drugstore" loads of multiple grades of clean petroleum products. My experience in that trade was very helpful in these discussions.

I enjoyed working with Moran's excellent Engineering Department, run by Eugene F. Moran. They were able to come up with a design having all the things I wanted of a barge along with the price estimates from several shipyards, so we could calculate the daily cost to operate. She was going to be a larger version of the Esso Tow No. 1, capable of holding 25,000 barrels of various grades of clean products. Mr. Moran gave the go ahead to build that barge (later to be christened Delaware). The contract was awarded to Todd Shipyards in Houston, Texas.

It was agreed that the tugs to be used on my operation would be transferred out of the Curtis Bay fleets with one a bit larger to handle the heavy oil barge, later to be christened "New Jersey."

This would insure no connection whatsoever with Local 333.

The final part of the new company launching was a new name. I suggested "Transitoil Corp." and it was accepted.

While all this Company business was going on, Marion and I were enjoying living in Crofton. We did however, plan Michael's Baptism and party to be held in Long Island, NY, since Jack Fitzgerald and Carol Jacobs were going to be the Godparents.

Many of our close relatives wanted to come visit us in Maryland, and they did, so we spent many weekends enjoying being tourists in Baltimore, Washington, DC and Annapolis. There was so much to see. You could spend an entire year exploring Washington and still not see it all. The Capitol city of Annapolis and the US Naval Academy, each were a wonderful day trip as was Baltimore and if you liked seafood, it was heaven. We really enjoyed our neighbors as well. I played on the local men's softball team and assisted coaching with Paul's Little League team. We hosted a going away party for our next door neighbor, the pilot, when he was being transferred to fly out of Miami, FL. While at the party, I had asked him how the move was going? He said: "Everything is going smoothly, except I can't find a home for my daughter's horse." I'll admit that maybe I consumed one or two too many Martinis. "Oh! I would love a horse, I used to ride a lot growing up in Brooklyn." When I woke up the next morning, the moving truck was there vacating their house and a horse was tied to a tree in our front yard. The pilot and his family were already gone, so there was no one to say "Hey, I was only kidding." It turned out that the daughter hadn't ridden the horse for awhile, so after being thrown twice, I gave it away to a farmer.

Ours was a popular place to visit with us hosting Jack and Carol, Evelyn and Steve, Geraldine and Dennis a lot and my brother Don and family, my Mom, John and Carol Jacobs and Matt Daniti, not all at once. We loved having them and keeping families close.

The Gallaghers and us decided to do a different vacation that summer, while I was waiting for equipment to come on line. We chartered a 42' houseboat from a chartering company located on Kent Island, MD across the Bay from Annapolis. Chesapeake Bay is a wonderful place for cruising with great weather and many interesting ports to visit like Oxford, Cambridge, St. Michaels and of course Annapolis. We anchored in a cove one evening and Dennis and I had nets and a light shining down into the water. When a blueclaw crab swam by, we'd scoop it up. After about 15 minutes, Marion came out and commented: "Don't you have enough bait yet?" When she found out it wasn't bait we were netting, but the crabs that we eat, she grabbed her own net saying "move over boys." We got about 20 keepers, no females, and had a feast that night. The next day, we heard that schools of striped bass were in the neighborhood, so we began trolling lures behind us. I was wondering why all the other boats fishing seemed to want to get close to us. I didn't know what they were thinking because I had no special tricks to catch fish. When I saw the binoculars looking over at us I got the hint. I went up to the top deck to see Geraldine sunbathing in a skimpy bikini. I never said a word and went back below. The whole trip was a fun memory.

Another good thing happened while living in Crofton, MD was the rekindling of a friendship with Pat Manning who was dating a Navy Captain named Bill Dougherty. Pat and her ex were good friends with Jack and Carol going back to living in Bay Ridge Brooklyn where we all grew up. Captain Dougherty was an Annapolis grad and pulled an assignment for a short period at the Academy. Marion and I's fondest memory of that time was attending Mass in the Academy Chapel and hearing the Navy Choir sing there. Pat and Bill also got married during that time and Pat asked Marion to be her Maid of Honor. It was the beginning of a lifelong friendship. Dennis and Geraldine's visits sparked some very fun parties. The six of us actually did a weekend in the Pocono Mountains at Strickland's Resort. One funny story while there……..on a late night search after partying, we found an indoor pool where there was no one around. We thought at the time, a little skinny dipping would be fun. After all there was no one to see us, so it would be fun. Little did we know that hidden security cameras caught our entire act out at the check in desk of the hotel. It attracted quite a crowd we heard.

During all this time, Transitoil Corp. was coming to life with the delivery of the brand new barge New Jersey and the new Curtis Bay tug conversion, the tug Accomac. The name came from a Delmarva Peninsula town on the Eastern Shore. She was big and a good match for the barge. Crewing the vessels was easier because of our contract with the SIU union. It was felt that it would be better for me to operate out of an office rather than from home and I couldn't agree more. There was a one room office available upstairs from Curtis Bay's offices that fit the bill. All of Transitoil's business accounting was going to be handled by the Curtis Bay's accounting department, leaving me to concentrate on sales and operations.

Gulf oil Co. employed the New Jersey for her first three voyages with Hess Oil Co. following right behind. The Gulf voyages were ship lighterings, loading from an anchored ship and delivering to various small Gulf Oil terminals. Hess wanted a full load of #6 oil delivered to their Washington, DC terminal from their Curtis Bay Terminal in Baltimore harbor. The Captain aboard the Accomac needed to be given his regular time off, so a new Captain was being supplied by the Union. He was to report to the vessel at Hess' Curtis Bay Terminal. Our regular Mate called and told me this new Captain appears to be "under the weather" and when the Mate helped him with his luggage to board, he noticed one bag was full of whiskey bottles. I packed a small bag and told Marion that I would be home in a couple of days. Upon my arrival it was obvious that "under the weather" barely described his condition. We removed him from the tug, called for a taxi and got him off of Hess' property. So, I was back being a tug Captain, something I always found enjoyable, especially for my first trip up the Potomac River. When I was docking the barge at Hess' terminal on the Anacostia River, near Washington, the new relief Captain was waiting on the dock and he turned out to be a good one. I stayed with the unit until we returned to Baltimore and got a good look at the new Captain's abilities.

The most important thing that happened while in Crofton in 1972 was satisfying a constant desire by Marion. When she was a teenager in Brooklyn, she volunteered at an orphanage and got so depressed that the policy at that time was that they could not show any loving gestures toward these babies and it killed her. She swore that if possible, she wanted to adopt a child out of an orphanage. We met a couple at one of her brother Jack's parties who had recently adopted a beautiful little girl from South Korea, so Marion got all the information from them on how it was done. We already had three boys, so going ahead with this was definitely going to be a girl. Catholic Charities pointed us towards Holt Adoption Services who were the principal agency working in South Korea. It took awhile to make it happen with all the tests that we were put through and the home inspections from Catholic Charities. In the Fall of 1972, there was a major typhoon heading right for South Korea, so Holt Services decided that they would put all the babies who were approved for American parents, on one airplane and send them off before the storm would hit. That plane's first stop enroute to New York City was Anchorage, Alaska. When U.S. Health Officials boarded the airplane in Anchorage, they deemed it a health hazard to have 320 babies on one plane, so Holt had to charter a second aircraft to complete the trip to New York. We were told to head for LaGuardia Airport and wait for the arrival. You can imagine the anxious feelings of 320 expectant parents and their friends and relatives mulling around that one section of the Arrivals section in the airport. We made friends with another couple who were expecting an eight year old girl and we all were so excited. When they finally opened the door, a young man came out holding an infant over his head and yelled out, "I have the McVay baby here." It is hard to express my feelings at that moment but Marion's elation and sense of fulfillment just permeated the joy we all felt. Jack and Carol were there to share in the moment. We already arranged that beautiful little Kim Mi Quan would now have her official name to be Christine Mary McVay.

The couple we befriended were told that their girl was on the second plane to arrive, so we went with them to the other Airway to wait with them. To see a little eight year old girl, dressed in the traditional Korean formal wear, come out and meet her new parents and then reach behind her to retrieve and present a flower arrangement to the woman saying "MaMa"……………….. There was not a dry eye in the place.

Even though the pick up kept us there until 10:00PM, we chose to drive home for 3 hours just to be ready the next day.

The barge Delaware's construction was completed and Marion was chosen to do the honors of christening her in Todd Shipyard's, Houston, Texas facility. It was a fun couple of days complete with champagne crashed on the hull by Marion, followed by brunch at Brennan's restaurant. "Breakfast at Brennans" is a famous place in New Orleans and the Houston version runs a close second. Arthur Stout, the President of Todd remembered me from the meeting with Tom Moran over the barge Chemical No. 1.

Bob Williams of Esso was true to his word and had work for the Delaware as soon as she arrived in the area. The workload doubled, especially training new barge crewmen in the complexities of transporting multiple products without downgrading any of them during the discharge. Between Bobby Hague and myself, we got it done to the satisfaction of the customer and ourselves.

Gulf Oil Co. and Hess Oil managed to keep the New Jersey working steadily and Esso did the same with the Delaware.

The McVay household was also a very busy place, especially with our new arrival. Christine became quite ill in those first few days at home that culminated in her developing a 106 degree fever and a rush to the Emergency Room at the hospital. Thank Heavens Dennis and Geraldine were visiting that weekend so we had someone to watch the other kids while we rushed off to the hospital. We actually had her in an ice bath to keep that temperature under control. It took a Chinese doctor to identify the problem: apparently Christine was never fed dairy products in Korea and as such, she never developed the electrolytes in her digestive tract to handle milk. We fed her just like we fed the boys turning out to be the opposite of what we really should have done. Fortunately, several injections of electrolytes and few day of observation in the hospital, seemed to resolve the problem. When she got healthy and Marion dressed her up in the cute clothes she bought for her, there was no denying that she was a beautiful baby girl.

There were major things going on at Moran Towing in New York. The Company moved its Corporate Headquarters from 17 Battery Place, home for over a half century or more, to the newly constructed World Trade Center, 5335 One World Trade Center to be exact.

Tom Moran, now Chairman of the Board and President of Moran, was making some serious changes in the office personnel with many Moran family connected employees retiring or being encouraged to move on. One of those was Frank Belford who ran Seaboard Shipping Co., the oil barge division.

There were rumors that I might be transferred up to the home office in New York in some capacity. That was very sad news because Marion and I LOVED living in Maryland. We were lamenting the possibility to our friends, Bob Williams (Esso) and his wife, one evening when we invited them to dinner at our house. The next day I received a surprise phone call from

Bob suggesting that if I would leave Moran to stay in the area, he might have something for me. He of course knew my record of working for Esso in New York and that his current Tug captain and docking pilot for Baltimore harbor was going to be retiring shortly. He did not have a replacement. I was so intrigued with the idea that I actually went and rode on his tug for a couple of days and rode on the ships with his pilot.

Before I had a chance to make any rash decisions, I got a call to report to Mr. Moran in New York promptly. This turned out to be a little deja vu with the first time I was going to quit Moran. With the Esso deal in my back pocket so to speak, I sat down with the Man to listen to his plans.

He explained the reshuffling of personnel that included Frank Belford retiring after 20 years running Seaboard and that it left him with no one to run the entire barge division. He said that since I was his oil barge expert in the Company, that he wanted me to be the Manager of Seaboard Shipping overseeing all 20+ pieces of equipment. He wanted me to sell my house in Maryland and move to the New York area as quickly as possible. The salary was going to be commensurate with the increased responsibility and the higher cost of living in the area. I forgot the deal in my back pocket; New York, here we come.

CHAPTER 28

Once again we could take advantage of inflation in the real estate market, having purchased our Crofton house for $47,500 a mere 2 ½ years prior. We got to sell it for $64,000 leaving us plenty of room financially, to find a comfortable home in the New York area. The husband of the couple who bought it was a general contractor and raised beagle puppies as a hobby. I had built a nautical themed bar in the den of that house. It had a 55 gallon fish tank built into the front of it and a pair of red and green brass ship running lights inserted in each corner. It was the nicest thing I ever built. When the husband saw it, he asked if the bar was staying with the sale and when I said yes, he literally told his wife to go look at the rest of the house. If there were enough bedrooms, they would take it and they did.

I realized what a wonderful bride I had the good fortune with whom to fall in love. With four kids, two of whom were really still babies, a house in an area we really loved and then to accept so easily that the Company wants us elsewhere, so let's go. It was so wonderful to be so fortunate.

While thinking about where we wanted to live near New

York City, we did not want to have to deal with the traffic of Long Island, nor the congestion of living in the City, so we decided to look in New Jersey. At the time there were tax advantages to living in New Jersey.

In our search, we came upon Manalapan Township, NJ where new homes were being built into an established community. We found a brand new house that was just completed, with four bedrooms and a back yard that was a bit odd in shape but big enough to install an 18' x 36' inground pool. It was not the smoothest of moves by a long shot. First off, as we were leaving Crofton, the new owner of our house came out and plopped a beagle puppy in Paul's lap and said it was a gift our kids should have. When we got to New Jersey, there was no moving truck with our belongings, so we had to move into a two bedroom unit in a nearby motel. Having a beagle puppy, by then named "Pepper" added to the confusion. The moving company we hired for the move, Global Van Lines, lost our truck for over a week. It seems that the two drivers went on a drunken spree and wound up abandoning the vehicle in upstate New York near Kingston. Fortunately, the truck was never vandalized and stayed intact. It was not a good week for a family with four young children. There was a Diner attached to the motel so food was not an issue. The Diner staff adopted our little family, helping out where they could, and that made things easier. With Paul 10 years old and Scott at 7 years we were fortunate that the Catholic Church near us, Christ the King in Old Bridge, NJ, also had a very good elementary school attached that had room for the two of them.

Prior to heading North, I had to close down Transitoil. Gulf Oil and Esso would miss our little operation, but when you are that big, you can adjust easily. I had both barges towed to Perth Amboy Drydock to paint them out to the Seaboard colors. Artie Blum was the Port Engineer for the Seaboard fleet and he and I had become very much acquainted with all the help he gave me starting up service with two brand new barges.

When I made my debut at Moran's new office at the World Trade Center I was surprised to see that the flooring in the lobby was not yet installed. Wooden walkways had been built to get people to the elevators. With Moran's office on the 53rd floor, you had to take an express elevator to the 44th floor, then a local to the 53rd. The express elevator went exceptionally fast and when I exited that car, I got a nose bleed. Apparently it was common until they adjusted it to go slower.

The Seaboard office people looked at me with trepidation, my being the same person starting a just a couple of years ago. None of them knew about Bartran or Transitoil. With Frank Belford gone, I guess they wondered who's next? In my meeting with Tom Moran, he made it clear that Seaboard was going to be my responsibility and as such I could keep or let go anybody while shaping my Division. The truth was, Seaboard was doing basically okay with only tweaking necessary to make it more profitable. There were a few old customers who's work was only marginally profitable at best. I was actually quite lucky having Jim Sheeran, an elder gentleman, who knew the division well enough to keep it running smoothly on a daily basis. Stuart Mortenson took care of our biggest customer, Northeast Utilities, to whom we transported #6 oil to their generating plants for Connecticut Light and Power and Hartford Electric. We also managed the coal barges delivering coal to the Norwalk power plant. Stu was in daily contact with each power plant and maintained their inventory of fuel for them. I was so lucky to inherit one of the best secretaries in the Company, Cathy Tarpey, who made my transition into the office very smooth indeed. Cathy was Frank Belford's secretary and really had a handle on the business.

My office on the 53rd floor had windows facing South with

the whole upper bay of New York harbor visible. Next door to my office was the dispatchers office, the hub of the New York operation and with occasional listening, I kept abreast of everything going on in tug operations. On the other side of the dispatchers was Malcolm MacLeod's office, Manager of Harbor Operations. The big office at the far end was home to Captain Leonard Goodwin, Vice President Operations. There were 25 tugs calling New York home. The tugs involved in ship assists, docking and undocking, as well as local barge movements came under the supervision of harbor operations. The bigger tugs involved in movements that were coastwise or ocean going were Captain Leonard's charges. They included the big cement barges, coal barges and rescue operations with which I had much experience. Captain Goodwin worked for Admiral Moran back during their WWII operations at Normandy. He actually remembered me from the time the Harriet Moran was off Fort Pierce, Florida and got a towing line caught in her propeller. I dove with mask, fins and a hacksaw to free the line. Captain Goodwin and I spoke the same language regarding operations, so we got along just fine. That was not the same with everybody, with some people being lambasted by the good Captain with some very colorful language. Tom Moran introduced me around as Captain Russ, so that name stuck.

Marty Carroll was the Vice President under Tom Moran and he was the contact to the Vice President, Fuel Supplies at Northeast Utilities. Shortly after my arrival, it was made clear that I was to develop a close relationship with this customer, a very large customer indeed. We sold them the idea that Seaboard was their transportation company and as such they were not stuck with one oil supplier. Companies like Hess Oil Co., who had their own barges and tugs, wanted to quote prices that included the transportation, but that would make Northeast a captive to Hess. Our relationship worked well for them and I made frequent visits to them in Connecticut to help maintain that relationship.

We actually capitalized on that relationship and used it to land a contract with Orange and Rockland Utilities, located in Haverstraw Bay on the Hudson River. I convinced Mr. Moran that we could keep two new barges busy to satisfy Orange and Rockland Power Co. and to bring larger loads to the Montville, CT for Northeast Utilities. Thus we got the barges Maine and Rhode Island built at 64,000 barrels capacity each. We sold off the older, smaller, original Seaboard barges leaving a fleet of dedicated newer equipment that turned a profit.

The rest of the 1970's was filled with great things both at home and the Moran office.

CHAPTER 29

During the early 70's, we began seeing American flag tank vessels dropping out of service simply because of age. The Jones Act stated that only American flag vessels can transport American goods from one American port to another American port. Goods included oil. Moran responded by building a 30,000 Ton clean products barge to fill that gap transporting clean products from Gulf Coast refineries to East Coast distribution terminals. The economics were there, having a 30,000 Ton barge with a 5000 HP tug and a crew of 9 vs. a 35 to 40,000 Ton ship with a crew of 44 officers and men. The barge New York with the Joan Moran was a unit supervised by Captain Goodwin.

Around the same period, Moran bought Florida Towing Co. of Jacksonville, FL, expanding the Moran companies further South on the East Coast.

The Connecticut Power and Light Co. decided to switch their Norwalk Connecticut plant from coal to oil and we were asked to supervise the conversion of one of their coal barges to one that would carry heavy oil. Arthur Blom of Seaboard was a supervisor of that conversion working with Moran's Engineering

Department. With the conversion, the Sea Horse 1 was our first double hull barge in the oil trade.

As Manager of Seaboard, I was given a membership in the Downtown Athletic Club located several city blocks south of the office. I remembered that when I was a stock boy for Rogers Peet Clothing, age 15, I would accompany the senior sales man carrying samples to the DAC. Executives would come to a room where we were set up for fittings for the suits they ordered. And now, here I was, a member.

I chose that one or two days a week, I would play four wall handball to help stay in shape. I played against FBI agents along with a collection of others there for the same reason. One day, there were no opponents available, so I was just playing alone for exercise when the back door to the court opened and in walked a very large man. He was super nice and he said he'd never played the game before and could I teach him. After ten minutes of rules and the basics we started to play. Game one: I won 21 to 6. Game two was a little harder with a victory of 21 to 14. Game three, he slaughtered me 21 to 3. I thanked him for the games and left. It turned out that he was Irv Cross, who played corner back for the Philadelphia Eagles. It was a very humbling experience.

The Downtown Athletic Club brought together many of the Principals of the tugboat community of New York. For me, I got to meet the owners of most of the tugboat and barge companies and found them to be friendly competitors. I met several McAllisters, including Brian. I reminded him of our first encounter on the SS Flying Fish where he did a Chesterfield cigarette commercial. I got to know his Dad and his Uncle, Anthony and J,P. McAllister. Others who were frequently there were Harold and Franklin Reinauer, Bart Turecamo, Janet Poling, Morty and Fred Bouchard, Doc Feeny and Frank Bushey. Mr. Bushey owned

Spentonbush and Red Starr Towing where my father worked. The irony of that encounter did not escape me.

Managing the Seaboard fleet of barges was actually quite a lot of fun for me. My management style was "hands on" so at least once a week, I was out of the office visiting one or two of those barges while loading or discharging. All of the crews got to know me and my having done that job myself, I knew the right questions to ask. I was actually very pleased with the crews we employed. I never left my inspections to just the barges, so I checked on the tug crews towing our barges as well, when they were there.

It was as a division manager that I got to know the Moran method of how each division was charged for each piece of equipment and therefore how to work up rates quoted to customers. Moran Corp., the parent company, would charge charter hire for each day a division operates a piece of equipment. It was up to us to meet that charge with earnings and beyond to make a profit for the division and keep the parent company whole. It was a bit of a handicap sometimes when competing against other companies who were not as sophisticated using a system like ours but overall it worked well and kept the parent company strong.

Meanwhile back on the home front, Marion and I were setting up our household as this was going to be our house for a lot of years, as opposed to what we have been doing for the previous years since we were married. Englishtown, NJ in Manalapan County was ideal for families with young children because there were lots of kids in the neighborhood. When it became known in the neighborhood that Mrs. McVay was friendly and welcoming to other kids and that we had a pool, 25 Arbach Lane became a very popular hangout for kids. I came home from work one day and counted 18 kids in our pool…..MARCO…. POLO……. splash!

Paul and Scott were performing well at Christ the King Elementary School in Old Bridge and Marion and I became experts in BINGO, since working Bingo games for the Church was a requirement for having your kids attend the Parish School. The Church had four games per week.

Marion and I had plenty of people to socialize with in the neighborhood, plus we were fairly close once again, with the Fitzgeralds, the Carbones and the Gallaghers. That closeness was especially nice around the Holidays where the 12 cousins, all our kids, continued to develop their close relationships.

Moran continued to upgrade its fleet of tugs adding new classes of tugs with greater horsepower to satisfy the necessities of customers introducing bigger and bigger ships. During the 1970's, container ships were the growth maritime industry.

The significant year for me was 1976 where a lot happened in the New York office. Malcolm MacLeod was sent to start up a new division in Ponce, Puerto Rico. He was given a tug and the barge Chemical No. 1 to be used transporting chemicals from the refinery in Ponce around the island to a distribution terminals in Mayaguez and Guanica. This was hopefully going to open the door to additional business on the Island.

With Malcolm's departure, I was appointed to be Manager, Harbor Tug Operations and would keep being Manager, Oil Barge Operations. W. Anthony Watt (Tony) was to be transferred from Florida Towing Corp. in Jacksonville, FL and he was told that he would be Manager of the Oil Barge Division. A funny story came out of this situation. I got called into Tom Moran's office and Tom seemed perplexed. He told me that he had Marty Carroll tell Tony that he would be Manager, but now, since he really didn't know Tony that well and wasn't sure whether he would like him or that he could do that job, he wanted me to tell him that he'd my assistant Manager. Tom said he hated to fire Managers. Not knowing what to expect, it was up to me to break the news. When I told Tony he'd be my Assistant Manager, not Manager, Tony's response was: "You can call me a son of a bitch, I don't give a shit about titles as long you don't reduce my pay." I knew from then on, Tony and I would become the best of friends.

Tony had plenty of barge experience having grown up business wise at Spentonbush Barge company and Bushey's Shipyard, so he eased right into the Seaboard fleet. It was a good thing since now my responsibilities increased a great deal. A fleet of around 20 tugs doing not only ship assists, but also barge movements, dredging projects and oil barge movements for other barge companies introduced a whole new cadre of customers to get to know. An additional responsibility included Moran's Docking Pilots.

I'll never forget the first meeting I called for with the Pilots. Remembering when I worked on the Moran tugs, the docking pilots were held to the highest esteem earned by many for their skills in ship handling. Now I was 34 years old, a good 10 years younger than the youngest of them and was the Manager to whom they reported. Our meeting started with one wise crack: "So CAPTAIN, what is it you bring to this meeting?" I hesitated, not expecting the question, then my response: "Well, I guess I bring experience. How many of you mastered the engine room signaling system on a Bell Boat when you were 12 years old?" I told them about my summers with my Dad adding, "steering a tug with two barges on gate lines behind us, using charts and aids to navigation." I went on: "I know you all know about Mariner

Class ships, 21 knot ships with 7 hatches and that US Lines has a few. The Pioneer Muse was my first ship as a Cadet, age 19, at the US Merchant Marine Academy. We got caught in a typhoon in the Western Pacific and got washed up onto a coral island. The ship broke in half and we scrambled off the bow using a Breecher's Buoy that I helped rig and after a day and night ashore got rescued by Navy helicopters." I continued: "In my second part of my sea year as a cadet on APL's President Monroe, a ship you all know, on a Westbound, round the world voyage, the 3rd officer died in Yokohama. When they couldn't get a replacement right away, the Captain made me 3rd Officer. At 20 years old, I was in charge of my own watch on a cargo/passenger ship for 2 months. After graduation from Kings Point, I sailed as 3rd Officer again, only this time with the license, on a 4 month trip around the world Eastbound, after which I came to work for Moran and sailed on every tug with an M on its stack. I also worked at Esso and by age 25, I was Captain of the Esso Massachusetts where I grew my First Class Pilots license, any gross tons, to as big as any of yours. I also rode ships with the Esso Pilots and learned many of the skills that you exercise on a daily basis. The biggest thing I learned was that Moran's Pilots are the envy of everyone in our business and are clearly recognized as the very best group of Pilots. So, that's what I bring to this meeting." There was not a peep for a few moments. Future relations with the Pilots was always pleasant.

My commute to the office consisted of my driving to Jersey City, then taking the PATH train right into the basement terminal of the World Trade Center. PATH = Port Authority Trans Hudson. Moran's "yard" was a pier in Port Richmond, Staten Island on Arthur Kill waterway. The yard was the central depot for the harbor tugs, used for crew changes, picking up supplies and generally "hanging on" between jobs. Several times a month,

I would find out which tugs were at the yard and then I'd stop there enroute to the office to talk to the Captains and crews giving them a voice to the management. Many of the crew members, I'd already known from my time working the tugs.

Every once and a while, I remembered my Dad's words: "Moran is the best" and here I am managing the entire New York fleet, trying to keep it that way.

New York Harbor was often the place to celebrate some happy events. New ship arrivals usually meant a parade of tugs and the New York Fireboats shooting huge sprays of water from their on deck water cannons. Also, on rare occasions, there were mega-celebrations that involved the entire New York City. One such celebration was our nations Bicentennial on the 4th of July, 1976. The United States was 200 years old on that date and sailing training ships from all over the world formed a parade of tall ships to help celebrate this day. I got heavily involved in the planning, especially since we had the US Navy contract that year to assist all their ships in the harbor and there were quite a few. I was able to invite my brother and his family to join me on my tug. Don and his oldest and Marion, Paul and Scott actually came, leaving our house before dawn to be on our tug and in position when the tall ships proceeded up the bay from their staging area below the Verranzano Bridge. The US Coast Guard's sailing training vessel EAGLE led the parade followed by a string of nine of the most beautiful ships on earth and we were right there, up close. It was the first time that I saw the Fireboats spraying red, white and blue water salutes up at the front of the parade. It was a truly wonderful, patriotic display that I'll never forget. My brother Don and his kids were thrilled and said it was a day they would never forget.

CHAPTER 30

Life in Manalapan, NJ was quite nice, being relatively close to many good destinations. Ocean beaches from Sandy Hook to Seaside were less than an hour away. New York City and all its attractions were very do able. We established a family tradition that was repeated for a lot of years. At Christmas, we all went to New York City, first to Rockefeller Center for the wonderful decorations and of course, the tree. We then took in the Christmas Show at Radio City Music Hall. We followed that with a trip to the Rainbow Room for refreshments and a spectacular view of the Manhattan skyline. Finally, we topped off the day with dinner at Mama Leone's Restaurant, which was a special experience all by itself.

When Michael finally went off to Elementary school it left only Christine home with Marion. That provided the opportunity for me to give to Marion a Christmas present that she touted as being the best present ever. I gave her a one year, tuition paid, enrollment for Christine to attend the Yellow Duck Nursery in pre-Kindergarten classes. Now Marion had free time to do what SHE wanted to do. I was so happy to be able to do this for her. Christine actually loved being there to boot.

Manalapan offered excellent sports programs for the many children living there. Paul loved Little League baseball and played it well while in grammar school. We got Scott to try baseball, however, while his coach, Marion and I watched him sitting down in the outfield, picking dandelions, we agreed with him that baseball was not his sport. It turns out later that the sports activities that he loved were not team sports and that was fine.

As Manalapan was growing as a town, so were the sports programs, especially in baseball and football. There were enough kids in the football program to put 28 teams on various fields each Saturday. There was no need for Pop Warner programs.

Michael wanted to play football so we signed him up for the 6, 7 and 8 year old level. They were short of coaches and I got hooked into it. I was always a fan of football, but never played the game. I actually went to the library and found a book showing how to coach little kids in the game of football. When you put the helmet on some of these little guys, they looked like Bobble Head toys. It was actually a real fun experience, because as coach, I was out on the field with my team, the Dolphins, calling the plays and setting up the defense. Having players that age with such a short attention span was a challenge, but we taught the basics after I learned the basics. I found it to be really a lot of fun where the whole family got involved.

Working at Moran was easy because of the corporate culture that we were a "white hat" company, a term that meant no shady deals, no cheating and no sneaky beating the system. It makes corporate life easier knowing that if what you did was right and proper, you would never suffer any blow back. They didn't forgive stupid though.

The company was a very generous company as well. An example was, there was a charity in New York called the St. John's Guild dedicated to providing medical care for children whose life situations would not provide the opportunity to receive proper medical attention for anything. They actually built a 4 deck hospital barge and staffed it with dedicated doctors, nurses and aides, even dentists, covering all the medical disciplines. Different hospitals, orphanages and City run facilities for children would be invited to have their children come to the "Baby Barge" as we called it, to receive quality medical attention. Moran's part was to supply a tug to take the barge on an all day trip leaving from the West side of Manhattan to all around New York harbor. For some kids, it was the first time they had seen the Statue of Liberty or the New York skyline. The tour lasted from 9:00 AM to 4:00 PM, five days a week. Moran supplied the tug and Pilot and charged them nothing.

The Christine Moran with the "Baby Barge"

We had an exciting tow take place under the supervision of Captain Goodwin, VP Operations who secured a contract to tow two Naval vessels from Philadelphia's Naval Shipyard to the newly constructed Navy Park in Buffalo, NY. That included the coastwise tow to the St. Lawrence River, then navigating the many locks of the Seaway with two "dead ships" (no power) followed by the tow on Lake Erie to the park. Captain Goodwin had his top offshore skipper George Sadler and our very experienced Port Captain, George Minton to assist him. It went flawlessly. While my Department had nothing to do with the tow, I found it interesting that one of the Navy ships was the USS Five Sullivans. That was the ship, when as Cadets aboard Venture Galley, we flew our pirate flag to salute her. It happened when sailing near Newport, RI back in Summer Fun 1963.

An incident that did involve my harbor operations happened in 1977 at the shipyard that was the old Brooklyn Navy Yard on the East River. The yard had been reopened as a private Company that was building extremely large tank ships and had one near completion, the MT Stuyvesant, which was over a 1,000 feet long. On the night of July 1st, the Stuyvesant's tie up lines started breaking probably due to an extra high tide. As they broke, the gigantic hull started moving out of her berth into the East River. The Marion Moran was the first tug on the scene and notified the Moran dispatchers. I was notified, but Charlie Marshall, the chief dispatcher on duty, had the situation well in hand calling all the tug companies to see if any were nearby. They also used Channel 13 in that effort. Before they were done there were 7 tugs working to get this behemoth back in berth. The Diana L. Moran was the second to arrive and she had a Pilot aboard, Capt. Ray Carella, who took charge on scene. The Stuyvesant, aside from being so long and wide was also extremely high due to no ballast water in her. Had she gotten out into the East River, she would have probably taken out the Brooklyn Bridge with its 140' vertical clearance in the middle of the span and less, close to shore. The Manhattan Bridge would have been in danger as well. What a New York City tragedy that would have been, both from the Brooklyn Bridge being the oldest bridge and like a monument plus logistically destroying one or two main thoroughfares for cars, trains and pedestrians. It took into early afternoon before she was secured safely once again. We (Moran) received Letters of Commendation from both the Mayor and the Captain of the Port (USCG). Interesting note: one of the 7 tugs involved in this operation was Red Star's tug Providence, my Dad's old tug that had been recently repowered to 2,000 HP.

As the kids grew, we loved our town all the more. Paul graduated from Christ the King and got accepted into the very good Catholic high school, St. John Vianney as did many of his friends. Scott continued to succeed at Christ the King as did Michael.

Most of the team coaches in the town formed a men's softball team and asked me to join, an invitation I accepted. I played the position of catcher. An interesting side note: the team was short players and asked each of us if we knew anyone to play. By this time my in-laws, Geraldine and Dennis (Tapps) moved a couple of towns away and Tapps said he'd love to join us. I knew Tapps was quite an athlete although he didn't look it, he's a big guy. Some of my team were noticeably skeptical of him playing but were shocked in the first game. He was a lefty and played first base better than anyone on the team and was up 4 times and hit 4 home runs.

"Hey Russ, do you know any others???"

The tugboatman's mentality is closely related to that of firemen. The whole business of tugboating is geared to helping others as they assist ships to safely navigate harbors and dock and undock without causing damage. Tugs go out to sea to rescue ships experiencing difficulties like my rescue trip for the SS Havlom. We had another rescue that was classic. It involved a cruise ship, upon returning to New York from Bermuda she lost her entire propulsion plant off Point Pleasant, NJ, just south of the entrance to New York.

The generators did not fail, so the ship had lights and power for everything but its ability to move. We happened to have two of our 5,000 HP Heidi Class tugs available who immediately took off to help. Both tugs put hawsers to the ship's bow and began the tow around midnight. The ship towed easy due to her fine lines and when they got just below the Verranzano Bridge, two more Moran tugs made fast to the ship, one to each side. At 8:00 AM, her normal arrival time, the ship was placed safely in her berth on the West side of Manhattan. The Captain said that he kept the arrival party going a little longer than normal with drinks flowing. He swore that the passengers didn't even know that the tugs saved the day.

Another incident that further highlights my fireman theory took place when a major fire erupted on a Brooklyn pier where oil barges were tied up during idle times. There were five empty barges hanging on at the pier and they presented a potential disaster. Empty barges are more dangerous than full ones because of the fumes that are ignitable. Our tugs and a couple of others made fast to the barges and with water cannons shooting onto them to cool the decks pulled them out of the slip to Bay Ridge anchorage and safety. There were four Bouchard barges. The last barge out was our barge Delaware and she only suffered some paint blistering. The remaining tugs, ours included, stayed by the pier shooting all the water they could to aid the NY Fire Department's fireboats. Bouchard gave all the tug crews a nice bonus and a big thank you.

Life in the office at Moran was good. I was surrounded by people good at their jobs and happy to be there doing them. I became busy enough to justify my getting another Assistant and Everett Merrill filled that billet to a tee. He was a Moran dispatcher following years of working on the tugs. The Company had a service run by Everett, where we provided barges for contractors in Manhattan to dispose of construction debris (no floatables) without having to drive their trucks many miles out of Manhattan. When the barges at our dump site were full, we would tow them out to sea and dump the content. With just concrete and bricks, what we dumped was environmentally safe and we actually got requests from Long Island Townships to help create artificial reefs to improve fishing. Everett continued running that operation in addition to assisting me with all the daily necessities of keeping our Department running smoothly.

I found that as time went on, Tom Moran dealt directly with me on anything having to do with operations. Moran Towing in the late 70's and early 80's was in a position where we supplied energy cargoes, both coal and oil, for a good portion of the Power generating Companies in the Northeast. Because of that, we got an invitation to bid from Florida Power and Light to supply tugs and barges to move cargoes to their shallow draft Plants. We took it very seriously and sent a team to Florida to put together a meaningful bid. The Team of Malcolm MacLeod, Dick Roe, our Controller and myself visited every facility, using a rented helicopter to save time and meet the requirements. There was an incident with the helicopter when we were going to inspect the Turkey Point plant in Miami. Turkey Point was half Nuclear and half oil fired. We mistakenly landed on the Nuclear side and were met by a SWAT Team of armed guards who chased us away. We did move hastily to the oil side and everything went okay.

We submitted a very professional bid, but truthfully it was impossible to beat the company whose equipment was already there. What did happen though is that we opened a really good relationship with the Fuel Department of Florida Power & Light Co. We approached them with the same logic we employed with our Connecticut Power customers. "You should have your own transportation company, in case you run into problems with your supplier of oil."

We got them to agree to have us supply a large tug/barge unit that would transport their supply from Texas or New Orleans to Florida. I remember long discussions with Tom Moran talking about, if we are going to build this unit for them, we should really build two barges. That way we could go for a longer term contract, having backup in our barge capabilities. He agreed. The barges Texas and Florida had 130,000 bbls capacity with on board heating capability and state of the art equipment. It turned out that FP&L was transporting 44 million barrels of oil across the Gulf of Mexico each year and that kept our barges fully occupied.

CHAPTER 31

We had a neighbor, Rick, nearby who's house was on over 2 acres and he was a horse owner and had a coral in his back yard. Another neighbor, Bill McGrath and myself were also horse enthusiasts. When I was young, pre-high school and accumulated enough money from various jobs, one or two friends would plan a horse outing. Using the NYC bus system, we would travel out to Jamaica, Queens to the Jamaica Stables where we rented horses by the hour. It was a fun time for us riding alongside the Belt Parkway on the beach by Jamaica Bay, all for $1.75 per hour.

And now, there came a time that I saw an ad in the newspaper, that a stable that rented horses in New Jersey was going out of business and they were selling everything. Bill, Rick and myself went there one Saturday and the net effect was that Bill and I each bought a horse. For $300.00, I got a horse, a saddle and all the tack needed to ride. What a deal! My mare wasn't the best looking animal with her scraggy coat and one blue eye and one brown eye, but she could run like the wind. Another neighbor nearby boarded "Venus" for me for $50.00 a month. We had access to the fire trails that the town cut through the 10 square miles of forest nearby. One or two days a week, I would saddle Venus up and go for a run at 5:30 to 6:00 AM, before heading off to work. The three of us actually went to a couple of rodeos and I entered to compete in the barrel racing events. I never won anything but the thrill of rounding that last barrel and racing for the finish line was exhilarating.

After a couple of years coaching the youngest Dolphins, my next door neighbor begged me to take over as head coach of his team, the Cowboys, in the 9, 10 and 11 year old league. The sophistication of the game at that level came closer to high school football and I felt that I could not do the team justice with my lack of experience. The big saving grace was that the Cowboys assistant coach was going to stay. He did not want the head coaching job so I was it. As head coach, I was responsible for all the things like uniforms and equipment, the draft, team meetings and the offense. My assistant coach, Matt Coulson, had the defense. So, for me, it was back to the library and studying my new book, *How to coach high school football*. One sad thing about that level in this town league was that I could not have my own son on my team. Michael got drafted by the Bengals and their coach, Mr. O'Conner, hated the Cowboys for some reason.

One day in 1980, I was told to report to "the corner office" by Muriel Lewis, Tom Moran's secretary. I remember thinking, "Oh God! What's happened now?" Everyone seemed happy as I entered his office. Tom told me, "The Board of Directors voted today to elevate you to the position of Vice President, Moran Towing and Transportation Company. Congratulations." He said that the position would not change my job description very much, but instead it was a promotion for a job well done. I thought that was better than a change in my job and was happy to be awarded it. The first person I called was Marion, without whom none of this would have been possible. Having a totally stable home life with a partner who is so competent to keep things running smooth allows us both the opportunity to be the best we can be. We celebrated that night. The old saying that if you find a job that you thoroughly enjoy, you'll never work a day in your life and that applied here.

Coaching the Cowboys became a real labor of love. When my players went out on the field you would have thought that the Dallas team loaned them their pro uniforms. I really studied my "how to coach" books and that coupled with my assistant, allowed us to put a good team on the field. The kids, at that age, actually had quarterbacks who could throw fairly accurate passes opening up a new dimension to the kids game. Just before the season started, I was approached by a man who just moved into the neighborhood and had a son the right age to play. He was told by the league that the Cowboys were one player down and that he should find the Cowboy coach. The father timidly approached Matt and I hoping his son could play. There was one thing different in that his son was completely deaf. Oh my, where to put him? Matt and I were both the type that felt "this boy is going to play no matter what." It was Matt who solved the problem by suggesting to put him at the Center position. We devised a system where the quarterback would tap the Center's butt the number of times I had secretly flashed to him to hike the ball. It worked great!! At our first game, I got the Ref off to the side and told him that there would be a little extra movement in the backfield with our quarterback tapping our Center because the Center is deaf. I guess the ref got a little exited about that, causing him to go to the other refs saying, "There's going to be extra movement in the Cowboys backfield because their Quarterback is blind"…… HOLD IT!!! The boy was actually a good athlete so we used him on defense as well. He never was called off sides because he didn't move until that ball was hiked.

In the five years I coached we went to the Super Bowl three times and won twice. NFL where are you!! The year the Cowboys beat my son Michael's Bengals in the playoffs, I learned what it was like to have no one in the house speak to me for a few weeks and it was amplified because Christine was a cheerleader for the Bengals. To this day Mike reminds me of how he was deeply scarred getting beat by his own father. Yea right!!

CHAPTER 32

In 1982, Captain Leonard Goodwin, Vice President Operations, retired. He was a salty old sailor who was never bashful about unloading foul mouthed rebukes to those not living up to his expectations. Aside from that, Captain Len was an expert beyond comparison in the art of ocean towing and was respected worldwide for his knowledge of the field. His career with Moran lasted for 40 years and I was fortunate to be able to learn more from him for five years or so.

With his departure, I was given the addition on my title to Vice President Operations plus I got to move into the big office at the end of the Operations Department. My responsibilities now encompassed all tug and barge activities performed out of the New York office and the large tug/barge operations wherever they traded for a total of 25 tugs and a dozen barges.

New York City had decided that they wanted a salute to the US Navy by having the retired aircraft carrier USS Intrepid to be a tourist attraction. This ship was well known for picking up the Astronauts returning to earth during the Apollo missions. We won the right to tow her from Philadelphia to her permanent home at Pier 86, just below the Passenger Ship Terminal on the West side of Manhattan. I sent two big tugs to accomplish the tow, which they completed in very good time. When we attempted to put the Intrepid into her berth, she wouldn't go because the dredged out slip had filled in with silt from the river. We had to do something short of redredging. I remembered an old trick that shipyards used to keep their slips clear for their drydocks. The silt in the slip was the loose silt that flowed up and down the river with each change of tidal current. I ordered two 3600 HP, twin screw tugs to go up to the head of the slip with their bows into the bulkhead. Engines were set at full speed ahead and four 12 feet in diameter propellers created a washing current pushing the silt back out into the river where it belonged. The Intrepid eased in nicely after that.

We took delivery of a new 5,000 HP tug, the Doris Moran, and sent her on an epic maiden voyage with Captain George Sadler, our most experienced and capable skipper. After launching her at McDermott's Shipyard in Morgan City, LA, she went directly to Marinette Shipbuilding yard in Green Bay, Wisconsin, across the entire Great Lakes. She then brought her tow, two US Navy berthing barges, through the Welland Canal and then out the locks of the St. Lawrence Seaway. The first stop was Charleston, SC to drop off one of the barges after which she headed with the remaining barge to Long Beach, CA, through the Panama Canal. She returned to New York having completed the longest Maiden Voyage ever of over 10,000 miles.

I feel compelled to mention the names of all the wonderful people we were so fortunate to have in Moran Operations who kept things running so smooth. John Tedaldi, who was the main contact for all the offshore units operating outside of New York Harbor. John, and others I'll mention were very dedicated and meticulous in watching over their responsibilities. Everett Merrill kept eye on the harbor operations that were above the routine. It was rare for him to encounter problems that he could not resolve himself. Tony Watt, the "assistant" Manager of Seaboard Shipping had a great deal of shipyard management experience and was eventually promoted to run the Construction and Repair Department. Jim Sheeran continued to keep Seaboard running smoothly and profitably. Dan Grandone was our chief dispatcher and well respected expert of operations in New York Harbor. Bruce Richards, after working on the tugs, then graduating from St. Johns University came ashore working as a dispatcher following in his father Jack's footsteps. He was quickly promoted to work on chartering for our large barges. Bruce was responsible for introducing computers to the Operations Department. These people and others I haven't mentioned made Moran an enjoyable place to go to work.

CHAPTER 33

For the most part, my brother-in-law Joe did not keep in touch with Marion and I, nor my brother Don for that matter. Joe had hired a "housekeeper" to help raise his four children while he continued his NOAA career. When we finally did find out, we were shocked. Christopher, the oldest, graduated from High School and immediately joined the US Army just to get away from Joe and Marge (the housekeeper). Andrew went to his grandmother's house in upstate New York for the same reason. We also found out that the twins were in foster care homes. Through a series of fortunate circumstances for us, the 12 year old twins, Donna and Daniel wound up coming to live with us.

Going from a six person family to an eight person family went fairly smooth. We added a bedroom to our house and got the twins registered and attending school. Marion wished that when we had Donna as a baby we could have kept her.

Number three son Michael played two sports that he loved: football and baseball. He played baseball on the Town's Little League and then was selected to be on the All Star team, the team that was the beginning of the pursuit of the State championship.

His team made it to one game away from going to Williamsport, PA to play in the Little League World Series. It was so exciting to attend these contests and it became a real family affair. Christine helped as the team statistician. When the playing was over, I took the entire team and families for a sightseeing celebration around New York harbor on one of our newest tugs. They loved it.

We were approached by a movie production company wishing to charter a tug for some scenes in a movie they were producing. It was going to take place at the South Street Seaport on Manhattan's lower East side. We, of course agreed since this would not be the first movie in which Moran tugs "starred." When I found out that John Travolta and Olivia Newton John of *Grease* fame were going to be the stars, I got a novel idea. I asked our Christine if she would like to hang out with a couple of movie stars for the day. Of course it was yes at 10 years old. I checked with the tug Captain to see if it would be ok with him and he was happy to look after her. At lunch time, I went to the tug to check up on how Christine was making out. The tug crew loved her and took very good care of her. When I encountered Mr. Travolta, he looked spooked: "Who are you?" After that, he seemed like a pretty nice guy. Olivier was a sweetheart and so pleasant. At least when people ask have you ever met a celebrity, I have a good story.

During the 1980s, Moran continued to solidify its position as the major supplier of energy to the East and Gulf Coast Public Utilities. We had a superior fleet of barges, both bulk and liquid, matched with the finest, most powerful tugs.

New York harbor was witnessing a change that would continue for the foreseeable future. With the invention of containerization of ship cargoes, the traditional break bulk methodology became archaic and economically unsound. The piers lining the shores of Manhattan had slowly began to disappear with cargo centers moving out to the other boroughs and mostly to Port Elizabeth, New Jersey. We did participate in an elaborate waterfront party when the Brooklyn container terminal was opened. I remember going to a Maritime Society luncheon where the guest speaker was the often funny, New York's Mayor Edward I. Koch. He was explaining how he was being lobbied by environmental groups to allow the old piers in Manhattan to stay, since the local migrating "striped bass" fish schools have come to use the pilings as a good place to spawn. His response to them was warning of the fire hazards and the danger of rotting pilings to the harbor traffic. He also said, "With regard to the striped bass, I'm sure 'That Love Will Find a Way.'"

The new Brooklyn container piers would increase cargoes moving through the Port by 1 million tons. Port Elizabeth and Port Newark would surpass that shortly. We kept abreast with powerful, beautiful new tugs sporting that big white "M."

Word of my being named Vice President-Operations of Moran got out to Kings Point and they awarded me with a beautiful plaque saying "Outstanding Professional Achievement." It was presented at my Class of '64, twentieth reunion celebration. Every five years our class would come together to celebrate the number of years since graduation. John Mandel, a fellow graduate and I would put these parties together.

John and I did not know each other until 8 years after graduation from the Academy. John Ingram was a member of the Law firm that represented Moran for Admiralty law cases. I knew John Ingram since I was a teen and we both hung out at Breezy Point in the summers. Ingram approached me one day and said he knew one of my classmates, John Mandel. I never heard of him! I went home and looked in my yearbook and sure enough, he was there and it said he was from Brooklyn. Ingram set up a lunch for the two of us to meet, which we did at "The Windows of the World," a restaurant on the 114th floor of the World Trade Center. After only ten or fifteen minutes of questioning each other it turns out that were both born and raised in Brooklyn, that we both went to the same High School, Brooklyn Tech, and graduated in the same class plus we both were in the same class at Kings Point and never met. Just to explain, I was an Architectural Engineering major at Tech and he was College Prep, we had no classes together plus there were 6,200 boys at Brooklyn Tech. At Kings Point, John was the Captain of the swimming team and I was Captain of the Sailing Team, activities on opposite sides of the campus plus he was an Engineering major and I was Deck. This chance meeting was the beginning of a lifelong friendship, so thank you John Ingram. John Mandel was the owner of Mandel Security Co. which happened to have the Security contract for the World Trade Center. He and his wife Chris lived on their 300 acre dairy farm in upstate New York.

John and I made sure that we had lunch together at least once per month. It became more than that when we started doing things together like heading up the New York Chapter, the largest Chapter of the Kings Point Alumni Association, a task we accomplished for five straight years. At our quarterly luncheons, we would commonly have an attendance of 200 or more Kings Point graduates plus industry and Government leaders to be addressed on a topic of interest to us all. I remember one such meeting where John had arranged for US Congressman Mario Biaggi to be the guest speaker. Unfortunately, while enroute to the luncheon site, the good Congressman had an appendix attack and was rushed to the hospital. What to do??

I spotted a fellow in the audience, a fellow New Jersey resident who I commuted with from time to time, who was the tax expert for the Bank of New York. I asked him to step in and he gave a 45 minute oration on how to avoid a tax audit. For days, John and I were receiving congratulations on the wonderful event we held that day.

John and I also took over the task of Class Agent for our Class of 1964, a job where we were to keep our fellow classmates advised of the whereabouts and important things happening to the rest of our classmates. We did that for ten years, posting articles in the quarterly magazine, the Kings Pointer.

John and Chris put together a wonderful day of Olympics at their beautiful farm with events to compete for the kids and adults. It was a wonderful day and it showcased the magnificent farm that they had created. The barn for feeding and milking the cows was put together with the precision one would expect from an engineer. He had close to 100 cows milking and it was quite a sight to see the effort of getting them in the barn where they each had their space to stand and eat. While that was going on, the suction devises were attached to their utters and the milking began. A conveyor belt delivered their food and they ate on one end and then discharged their waste on the other end onto another conveyor belt that dumped the "farmers gold," fertilizer, onto a spreader to be taken out to the fields. John devised this amazing system. John also had horses, something I loved and we had many great rides around his beautiful estate. We had fun with an article for the Kings Pointer where we posted a picture of the two of us astride our horses. The article explained how we were on a cattle drive on John's property bringing the herd from the high country down to the low country for the winter. Many fellow grads envied the exciting lives we led. They, of course, didn't have to know that the distance from the high country to the low country on John's farm was about 300 yards. We laugh about that til this day.

On a cattle drive!

While riding, it was evident that there were too many deer on the property which destroyed some crops, so John invited me up to do a little deer hunting. It was the only success I ever had in that sport.

When we were at the Academy back in the 1960's, the Blue and Gray Club was the biggest donor to Kings Point Athletics and over the subsequent years since, it became less effective due to lack of leadership. We decided, with the help of two or three others, to revitalize the Club back to its former self. We came up with the idea of holding a golf outing in a local private Club but added an extra twist that really helped to raise funds. That twist involved holding an auction. Graduates who owned a time share that they weren't using, yacht owners offering a weekend vacation trip, owners of ski chalets offering a free weekend and many, many more. I offered a family day on a tug in New York harbor making it on a Saturday where the family would be on a tug undocking huge passenger ships. That went for $500.00. I recall that we raised a total of $54,000.00 on this our first try. Since then, the Blue and Grey Club has many golf outings with auctions every year across the country contributing hundreds of thousands of dollars to Athletics. We also raised enough to reopen the Athletic Hall of Fame which had suffered from lack of funds. John and I would continue to do things together and they all were fun.

CHAPTER 34

My view on being personally successful in business was to become indispensable as the Company expert in one or more areas of the Company's business. Mine was certainly for my experience and knowledge of the barge industry and equally with tugboat operations. When questions arose on those topics by anybody in the Company, the usual reaction was "ask McVay to join us in here." With that in mind, I was quite surprised by the next adventure set up for me.

Harvard University has a special program called the Advanced Management Program, offered to business executives who meet the following qualifications:

- Students must be at least 40 years of age;
- Must be at a minimum, Vice President of the Company who reports directly to the Chairman or CEO of their Company.

The tuition was $21,000.00 covering a 13 week program taken over two summers of 7 weeks for the first summer and 6 weeks for the final sessions. It was also offered in the straight 13 week term. The program was identical to Harvard's Master's, Business Administration (MBA) course tailored however to students who are already successful Corporate Officers. In our class of 140 students, more than half were from Countries other than the United States and represented business' in every field imaginable.

That summer of 1984 was set for me to take part in something that was unexpected but was also a great honor. I found out later that John Bull, past President of Moran Towing and Transportation Corp., Capt. Frank Hughes, Chairman of Curtis Bay Towing Corp. and Lee Christensen, CFO Moran Towing Corp. were those chosen to attend this Harvard program in the past.

The student body was divided into groups known as Can Groups of seven or eight individuals who would study together. MBA students in earlier times, had dormitories set up with eight small bedrooms surrounding one bathroom (or Can), hence the name "Can Group." The dorms had since been modernized, but the name stuck.

Boston was close enough to New Jersey, so I drove up to Cambridge to begin this new life experience. I quickly learned how fortunate I was to be teamed up with great people in my Can group.

The fellow across the hall from me was Pete Willcock of Three I's, "Investors In Industry," from London, England. Next was Zave Kuburski, CFO of the Equitable Life Insurance Corp. followed by Michael Meeks, owning partner of Holiday Inn hotels and Willie Fong of Smart Shirts Corporation. When I mentioned that I had not heard of Smart Shirts he touched the collar of my dress shirt and said, "You're wearing a Hathaway shirt probably bought at Lord and Taylor's." Smart Shirts manufactured 25 million dozen shirts annually and Hathaway was one of them. Phillippe Mattrapierre was Vice President of the largest producer of stainless steel in France. As I would eventually find out, this class was the who's who of business across the globe. An Indian Raja took over an entire floor of a nearby hotel to house the 23 people he brought along to cater to his every wish, including doing his homework assignments. We had Joseph Bassett of Bassett Furniture and Sam Wall of Walmart, and on and on. I thought I would be the only Tugboat person there, but I was wrong. The owner of a Ship Agency in Santiago, Chili also owned the harbor tug fleet in that port. There were loggers from Canada who owned and used tugboats to transport their raft of logs down the river to the mills.

On top of having top notch business people as the students, Harvard assigned some of their most well known instructors. Alan Dershewitz was our Law professor, George Cabot Lodge taught labor relations and on and on. It became obvious after awhile that these top level instructors not only taught this top level student body, but it was an opportunity for them to keep abreast of what is going on in business now.

This "college" experience was not going to include party time. Classes started during breakfast at 0730 and went on til 1700 (5:00PM) and went Monday through half day on Saturday. We used the "Case Study" method, just like the MBA course, examining companies and their practices while looking at their successes and failures.

We were off on Sundays and used the time to explore Boston. One local classmate was the Vice President of Operations of the Boston Aquarium and he hosted a cocktail party for all of us that was unique in that we had the entire Aquarium to ourselves. I got to know a fellow New Yorker, Dick Grasso, who would later become the President of the New York Stock Exchange and another New Yorker, Herb Whiteman, Vice President of the Federal Reserve Bank, "The Fed." The youngest classmate was Bob Pittman, founder of MTV, the music video company that changed the entertainment world for younger Americans. I thoroughly enjoyed meeting and working with on occasion, the only attendee from Japan, Masa Isogai. His Company was Safeway, the supermarket company, which I thought was an American operation. Safeway also owned Talbot's, the high end woman's fashion company. What was most interesting was that Masa told us that his company thought he should be married and that while he was at Harvard, his company was actively seeking a mate for him. I didn't think we would see that in America. He was such a humble gentleman, liked by all. He was also a smart businessman contributing positively to class discussions. There was one banker from South Korea and when I told him of our Christine being originally from Seoul, he wanted to know all about her. We spoke often. We had quite a few classmates from India with one being a Sikh. Sikhism, I discovered, is a religion originally from Punjab, espousing the best of Hinduism and Islam and while only 2% of the Indian population of 1.3 billion people, Sikhs are highly regarded among all Indians.

Those first seven weeks seemed to fly by quickly and now I had to return to my job and see what happened in my absence from the office.

I had come home from Harvard for one weekend because of Scott's high school graduation and Marion and I spoke everyday, with her keeping me abreast of everything happening on the home front.

The two summers that Paul went to St. Peter's College, he was looking for a job to keep busy and to make some money for himself. I asked, "How about working on a tug for the summer?" He said that he would love to do that. Our personnel manager, Ed Bachellor, helped him get his Seaman's Document and a Union card allowing him to work on our tugs.

Everyday, New York City's Department of Sanitation, transported approximately 26,000 tons of the City's garbage from dump sites located in all the boroughs, to the very large dump site in Fresh Kills, Staten Island. The towing contract required five tugs working six days per week to handle that monumental task. McAllister Towing and us had fleets to handle it and we would vie each year to see who would be awarded that contract. For the two years Paul worked aboard, the contract was ours. It was a good job for a new comer since there were two deckhands on every watch, so Paul could be with a very experienced partner to literally show him the ropes.

Spending each day on a tug, nestled between two scows fully loaded with garbage made you get used to the stink. That first week he came home, we asked how he liked it? "Flies are my friends," was the answer. Ugh!

During each of those two summers however, he earned enough to pay his college tuition and then some.

CHAPTER 35

When I returned home after that summer of 1984 at Harvard, it was great to be back with Marion and the kids. Paul was doing well at St. Peters College. His paternal grandfather, Matt Daniti, had passed away and left him a nice sum of money, enough to get himself a car. I had such good memories of "Mr. Daniti" from my earliest childhood onward. When my father died, he was my other Dad for things like father and son Communion Breakfasts and Boy Scouts.

Scott found out that he was accepted at St. Peters as well, so he and Paul were going to commute together. Michael, Donna and Danny were going to attend Manalapan High School. Mike joined the football team but as Freshman, he would be on the Junior Varsity. Donna tried out for Soccer with similar results as Mike. Christine was still in Grammar School and was a cheerleader for the Town football team.

Big things were taking place at Moran. From what I heard, Frank Belford, my first boss at Seaboard Shipping and a Moran stockholder, approached Tom Moran and stated he wanted to buy out the relatives and take over Moran. It happened that he did not have sufficient backing and money to make it happen, so he decided to withdraw. What his inquiry did do however, was light a spark in Tom's mind that he should buy out his relatives. The Moran stock ownership, like any in a Company that was 150 years old, was highly diluted with many owners having no idea of what goes on in a Tugboat company. Tom and Lee Christensen, the VP Finance, put together what was going to be a $100,000,000.00 leveraged buyout (LBO) matching the amount borrowed with the value of Moran. My contribution was to help assemble several established and reputable Marine Equipment Brokers who would examine each piece of our equipment and assign a value to them. We were of course looking to get a total value of Moran's various fleets of tugs, barges and real estate to satisfy Citibank, the lender. Citibank saw that the deal was going to be doable however, they justifiably were worried of what would happen to the Company if Tom were not there, for whatever reason. They wanted assurance that the Company would continue to operate per normal and still be able to payoff the loan. Tom identified those people who he would take as partners in the ownership of the Company, who would keep it running smoothly: Lee Christensen for Finance; Ned Moran, Tom's brother and seasoned port manager; Malcolm MacLeod for Management; Me for Operations and Tony Watt for Engineering and Sales. That lineup satisfied Citibank and the deal went through. It wasn't quite that easy as I remember sitting in room signing documents for hours.

 Life went on as it normally did, despite our new position in the ownership of the Company. I continued to oversee all the various operations. We continued to be the primary supplier of fuels to generating stations. We helped United Illuminating Co. in Bridgeport, CT to redesign its discharge pier facilities to fit our new barge Bridgeport. It made it economical to utilize low sulfur coal, a cleaner fuel. We also started delivering coal to the Fall River, MA generating station.

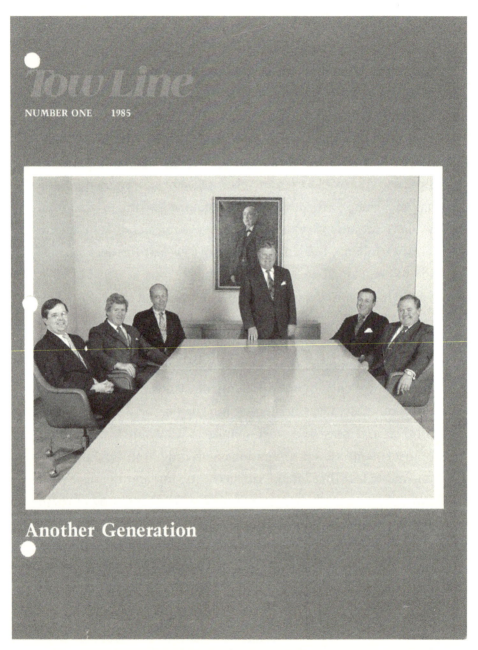

Business overall in Moran continued to run smoothly which was exactly what we hoped for. The plan laid out by Tom and Lee was to pay down the loan as quickly as we could. The new owners were committed to that and agreed to no pay raises for us until the loan total came down significantly.

In May of 1985, I had to return to Harvard for the second half of my Advanced Management course. Our first instructor welcomed us back and asked if anything significant happened to any of our Companies during the off time between sessions.

I raised my hand and was called upon where I said: "While we off, I took part with a group of the six top executives at Moran Towing Corporation, putting together a $100,000,000.00 leveraged buyout (LBO) and purchased the Company from the original stock holders." The entire class of 140 executives gave a standing ovation for several minutes. Even the instructor commented that he did not hear of anything like that in his previous experience teaching. I called Tom Moran and told him what just happened and he was happy to hear it.

We continued doing case studies of various companies and we also had presentations by new Company owners who wanted to run their business plans before such an audience. One such was the Italian owner of the clothing line known as Beneton, beautiful bright colored pieces for both men and women. The reception was positive. Sam Wall's Executive Assistant presented their plan of opening many stores (Walmart) and becoming the largest importer of a huge variety of items from China.

I invited our son, Paul to come to Boston and sit in on several classes, to give him an experience he otherwise would not be able to get. He thoroughly enjoyed it, especially getting to know my Can Mates. Paul was planning a trip to Europe with two cousins to visit another cousin living and studying in Paris. He got invitations to visit Phillippe in France and Peter Willcock in London. Phillippe loved Mexican food and couldn't get it in France and asked Paul to bring him some when he came. (He did). Peter took care of the cousins like they were his own children while in London.

I also brought Scott to Harvard and he also was in awe of the experience. He specifically remembers the marketing class where the Beneton presentation was made. Scott was a body builder and when he found the big exercise room in the dormitory, he used it. Some other classmates used it as well and Scott remembers working out with the future President of the New York Stock Exchange, Dick Grasso.

Around that time, it was Tom Moran's 60th birthday and his wife Miriam was hosting a gala party for him in a Country Club in New Canaan, CT. I was telling my Can Group why I had to drive to Connecticut and that I should get a hotel there where Marion could meet me. Mike Meeks handed me a piece of paper with the address of the Crown Plaza Hotel in Stamford and the hotel manager's name. Marion and I were never treated so royally in a hotel ever, including chocolates on the pillows and a bottle of champagne. I guess it helps to know the hotel owner. Tom didn't expect us to be there so he was happy and since he always had a special liking for Marion, he always had her sit next to him at any of the these social affairs because he loved chatting with her.

During the thirteenth and last week of the course, participants were encouraged to bring their wives to join them for the entire last week. I was amazed by how many complied, bringing their spouses from places half way around the world. Several hotels in the surrounding area were booked to capacity.

The camaraderie developed among us classmates was only

enhanced with the wives on the scene. Marion's favorite was Mike Meek's wife Claudette but we also enjoyed Mavis, Peter's wife, Zave's wife and Mrs. Willie Fong was a sweetheart. A tradition of the final week included that each member of the Can group would take the other members, plus wives, out to dinner for something special. Willie got right into it, locating a really good Chinese restaurant, reserving a section big enough for us all and he arranged the menu. Marion and I agreed, it was without a doubt the best Chinese meal we ever enjoyed. Phillippe took us to Maison Robert, the best French restaurant in Boston. When it came to be my turn, I surprised everyone. I called up a friend in Boston, Vincent Tibbets, President of Boston Towboat Co. and asked him if I could borrow a tug for an evening. He graciously said yes. The best seafood restaurant in Boston was Anthony's Pier 4 Restaurant actually located on Pier 4 downtown. Marion and I arranged for two limos to pick up our party and take us to South Boston to Boston Towboat's pier and yard.

My "Can Group" plus wives enjoying a tugboat cruise around Boston harbor and a great dinner I arranged. A beautiful night.

After embarking on their newest and cleanest tugboat (I complimented the crew), we were given a tour of Boston Harbor. It was a beautiful night and that made it even more enjoyable. After the tour, the tug docked on the end of Pier 4 where we entered the restaurant and were treated to a most delicious Maine lobster dinner. The tug actually waited for us, so when dinner was over we re-boarded the tug and enjoyed an evening cruise around Boston Harbor before being brought back to Boston towboat's pier to the limousines taking us back to the campus. They all agreed that this evening was the best and they never even dreamed that they would ever get to ride on a tugboat. My classmates said that they now had a hands-on feel for what my business entailed.

Bob Pittman, the founder of MTV, theatrical as he was, did a fun thing for the class. He hired a young woman who, while roller skating about the campus would interview each classmate throughout the week. Bob had a cameraman filming the whole thing as well. We each were presented a tape of the interviews, done with music, all very professional and quite hilarious.

Marion and the rest of the wives really enjoyed going to the classes with us. I know Marion felt that she had a better understanding and appreciation of why I was at Harvard and what we were learning.

Speaking of learning, I have to say that the entire experience gave me a better perspective on running a business as a whole. While studying different methods of running a business, there were many clues that could be applied at Moran Towing.

When I was back home, I kept in touch with a few classmates. A special surprise was getting an invitation from Dick Grasso for my whole family to come for lunch at the New York Stock Exchange. The kids loved it, especially the tour of the building and a walk out onto "the Floor" of the Exchange. It was so nice of Dick to do that for us.

I also got a call from Herb Whiteman Vice President at "The Fed" inviting my whole family for lunch and a tour. The tour down in the vault where different Countries store their gold reserves was amazing. We got hold gold bars and a million dollars of shredded $100 bills.

The entire experience was so enlightening and enjoyable at the same time. I feel proud that Moran selected me to attend such a prestigious experience.

In late 1985, Tom Moran decided that commuting to Manhattan to go to work for the past 35 years was enough. He decided to move the Company to Connecticut. It was not a unique idea since many Maritime Companies moved out of the high tax, high rent New York City locations out to Connecticut or New Jersey. The best indicator was going to the Downtown Athletic Club for lunch seeing so few Maritime people. There were mostly Investment and Finance people becoming the majority. Since many of the shoreside personnel working at Moran lived in New York City, Tom wanted to make the commute a less difficult one. Luck was with us when we located a perfect sized office right in the train station in Greenwich, CT. Greenwich was the first stop in Connecticut for an express train 30 minutes out of Grand Central Station.

Leaving the World Trade Center left most of us with mixed feelings. After getting over working in a building that creaked and groaned like an old wooden schooner in high wind situations, we became used to it. The spectacular vistas from the 53rd floor overlooking the Statue of Liberty and the whole Upper Bay of New York would be missed. That was especially true with our dispatchers, whose view would now be the Greenwich Railroad Station. I do not recall that anyone left Moran due to the move.

This development, of course meant that the New Jersey McVays, would have to move to Connecticut. The exodus of so many Companies from the high tax New York had driven the home prices in nearby Connecticut through the roof. We also had kids in elementary school and high school, so good schools were added to the equation. I had put a one hour commute time in the equation as well. After many trips and lots of study, Marion and I decided to settle in the Brookfield, CT area. It was a beautiful town with great schools and within the commuting time limit. The very large Candlewood Lake was on the West and Lake Lilinona to the East. We settled on a house with 2+ wooded acres and plenty of room for all of us. It was also within walking distance of the 12 mile long, Lake Lilinona, a dammed section of the Housatonic River. Marion's Mom, Grandma Mae, decided that she wanted to live with us and she handed me the keys to her house in New Jersey and said: "Sell my house and I'm going to live here." We had the room and she was a welcome addition.

Of course our new house would now would not have a living room since we converted that into Mae's little apartment. It of course also meant that we would have to sell our New Jersey house, a place where our kids grew up. We bought it in 1972 for $54,000.00 and now after too long a time trying to sell it, we were able to take advantage of inflation and sold it for $276,000.00. All of that went into buying the Connecticut house costing $375,000.00 which was by far the most beautiful house and property we ever owned. I knew it was the right one when Marion walked into the house and saw the kitchen, dining area, den and the wonderful forest view, she took a quick breath and said WOW!

It was not so well accepted by Paul and Scott who announced that they were not going to go to Connecticut which prompted me to go around and collect their car keys. I told them it won't be fun just walking around New Jersey. Needless to say, we had a three car caravan heading to Connecticut on moving day.

We had to register four children in Brookfield schools. Christine was easy since she was in 8th grade and only needed the second half to graduate. When we went to register our three high schoolers, Michael, Donna and Danny, we had to go to the school nurse who did the registering at Brookfield High School. The nurse asked if we had any athletes and we mentioned Donna was into Soccer and Michael played baseball and football. "What position does Michael play in Baseball?" When we said left handed pitcher, she disappeared behind a partition and we could hear her calling someone on the telephone. "We have a left handed pitcher moving in from New Jersey," she said. Obviously, she was talking to the Coach and you would think Cy Young just moved into the neighborhood.

With a personal visit to the Dean by Scott and I, we managed to get him enrolled in Western Connecticut Sate University. Paul finished up at St. Peters and was looking for a job in Connecticut. I had heard from our good customer, Northeast Utilities, that they may have openings in their Accounting Department due to expansion. Paul applied and was hired into their payroll department, a busy place with their 7,000 plus employees in five different states. It was nice to have all of our kids settled.

In a discussion with Tom Moran, he mentioned the limousine he had and no longer needed. I told him if he wanted it sold that I would sell it for him. He was happy to have one less thing to do. I took it home with me and as I was driving in our driveway, Marion was getting ready to leave. "I have to pick up Michael, he's late due to baseball practice." I said, "Wait, let's pick him up in the limo." We approached the school and saw Mike standing with his new team mates waiting for their ride home. I pulled up, jumped out and opened the door for him saying,

"I'm sorry to be late for you Mr. McVay," then closed the door and drove off leaving his team mates with mouths agape. He was upset, but we had a good laugh.

CHAPTER 36

In 1986, New York City decided to host the greatest celebration of the 100th Anniversary of the dedication of the Statue of Liberty. The weekend of the 4th of July was set aside with a nautical parade on that Saturday. First, the US Navy got involved with the arrival of the USS Independence and several of her escorts. Our good friend, now Vice Admiral Bill Dougherty, was the Fleet Commander based aboard the carrier. There was so much going on that we could not join up with him during this celebration. The parade would include every tall ship training vessel from a dozen countries, led by our own sailing training vessel, "Eagle" from the US Coast Guard Academy.

Anyone who owned a boat was invited to come to the harbor as spectators and it was estimated that over 20,000 boat owners initially responded. Corporations chartered all the Circle Line passenger boats and other charter fishing boats were filled to capacity. The Coast Guard and the NYPD marine fleet had all they could do to keep the lane open for the larger sailing vessels. The NYFD fireboats led the parade spraying red, white and blue water from their water cannons.

There were going to be two separate celebrations that day, the daylight session for the parade of tall ships and the evening session for the Liberty Island fireworks. We were going to use all of our tugs for each separate party. We catered each tug with lunch and invited many of our best customers and families to join us. We even rented the empty pier 42 East River as a staging place for boarding what turned out to be almost 900 guests. One of the nice things about now being an owner was that I got my own tug, the Miriam Moran. Tom Moran had his Mom with him and they were aboard her namesake, the Alice Moran.

My guests included customers with whom I had a personal relationship, as well as many family and friends. That was for the daytime session. Marion got a little lost driving down to Manhattan's Eastside. She was in the Bronx and finally asked a NYPD officer for help. The sergeant sent one of his patrolmen to give

Marion a Police escort right to the pier. How wonderful was that? After we had everyone aboard and then sailed out of the East River to the upper bay, the sight was the most spectacular thing I had ever seen: there was, as later estimated, over 30,000 watercraft in the Upper Bay, everything from a 1,000 foot Aircraft Carrier to 10 foot kayaks. We gently weaved our way out to the parade area. I guess 110' tugboats are pretty imposing and people on yachts moved out of the way. The parade of tall ships was a once in a lifetime experience. Each had their cadets manning all the yardarms as we watched in awe. It took almost 3 hours after which some of our tugs broke off to assist docking them at various Manhattan piers. Mayor Koch came by on a NYPD launch waving to the crowded onlookers.

When the parade was over, we made our way back to Pier 42 and disembarked those guests who were aboard for the daytime spectacle and got ready to board those who would join us for the evening fireworks. A great surprise was having Peter Willcock, my Can mate from Harvard, and his wife Mavis fly in "to the colonies" as they would say, to join us for the evening. I had invited Dick Grasso and Herb Whiteman but they had their own plans for the evening.

We went back out to the upper bay and it appeared that none of the vessels left and they awaited the fireworks show. We found a spot to watch and we were right alongside Forbes' 180 foot long "Highlander" yacht. We even saw a couple of movie stars aboard her. When the sun finally went down the fireworks started. We, at Moran, do the Macy's fireworks shows each Thanksgiving, towing the barges that launch the fireworks. We are used to seeing great fireworks shows. What took place on this night was the best show by far. They literally lit up the Statue of Liberty to look like a giant birthday cake with the 100 candles lit as well. It was breath taking and my guests loved it.

Watching the exodus of 30,000 watercraft from the Upper Bay, especially in the East River was an "Apocalypse Now" moment. Fortunately, Marion and I had a hotel room reservation right in Manhattan, so we didn't have to fight our way out of the overcrowded city.

Life in Brookfield, CT was good. The schools proved to be exceptional and our kids made a lot of friends quickly because they played sports. My brother Don and Cathy offered to help with the extra kids and Danny agreed to move up with them. Donna played Soccer and Michael was into football and Baseball. Christine went easily into the cheerleader program for Football and Basketball.

The baseball coach, Mike Cioppa, was excellent and the crop of players were really very good, especially the Cy Young award winning lefty pitcher who moved in from New Jersey.. We were right back to doing what we did with Little League, following the team around the region attending games where we could.

There was a restaurant nearby called the Taunton Tavern and Tugboat Lounge, so of course we had to go check it out. Sure enough the Tugboat Lounge had many pictures of tugs, but they were the wrong ones. We met and became good friends with the owners, Capt. Mike and Doris Bornyak. Captain Mike skippered the small tugs used to ferry equipment barges on jobs like bridge construction or repairs. It took me awhile, but eventually all the tugboat pictures featuring McAllister Bros. tugs were all replaced with beautiful photos of Moran tugs. Every one of our kids worked in that restaurant with Christine hosting, Scott waitering (working my way through college) and also Donna and Mike busing. Mike and Doris became lifelong friends, celebrating holidays with our families. Each Thanksgiving, we would have as many as 30 relatives and friends for Thanksgiving dinner, which became a tradition while we were in Connecticut. Great food and family games were the highlight. We even had a raccoon that would come to the back door and tap on the glass looking for handouts. The young kids loved it.

We took advantage of the giant lakes nearby and bought a 17' Starcraft runabout with a 90 HP outboard and a trailer, for water skiing and just fun exploring the lakes. I also would trailer the boat down to Niantic, CT to do some fishing with Paul. We would motor out to The Race, the fairly narrow spot between Long Island and Connecticut. It was a good place to catch big blue fish, and we usually did. Paul was very happy with his job, but it was a long commute to Hartford. He eventually found a room for rent, so he was the first to leave the nest. Scott did a semester at WestConn but took the opportunity that was presented to him to switch to the University of Connecticut (UCONN). GO HUSKIES!!

Following the Brookfield Bobcats was a traditional experience. Home football games were held on Friday nights, attracting most of the families with kids in the High School. Games under the lights, the band playing, the cheerleaders cheering with Christine out front, concession stands, families uniting all proved to be an exciting way to spend a Friday night. We had it all year with Mike playing both football and baseball. I remember commenting to Marion one Sunday that Mike plays in every game and we never see a picture of him in the newspaper. With that, I opened the newspaper to the sports section and there's a 12"x12" picture of Mike tackling a Newtown high school running back.

As much fun as it was going to football games, it was the Bobcats baseball team that was excelling in the District competitions. Michael was coming into his own as a left handed pitcher and first baseman when not pitching. He actually won both games of a double header each year, coming in as the relief pitcher in the first game and pitching the whole second game for the two wins.

June of 1988 was graduation, so we started looking for colleges for Donna and Mike. Donna set her eyes on the Fashion Institute of Technology. Marion and I will never forget taking her down to be interviewed and having the Dean telling Donna, "I know one course that you won't have to take going here….Dress for Success." Donna looked fabulous for the interview and with her good grades and resume' she got a full scholarship to attend.

Mike playing football

We took Michael to several colleges that had good baseball teams, Fairfield University, Villanova and the University of Rhode Island. Michael had some exposure to Kings Point from me and one day out of the blue, he decided that was his choice.

He had the grades and SAT scores to qualify and both Connecticut Senators gave him a nomination. He was notified he had an appointment to attend The United States Merchant Marine Academy starting in the summer of 1988. Marion and I were both so happy that he chose the Academy. The fact that he signed up for football meant that Marion and I could be with him earlier than the usual 8 weeks of quarantine for the PLEBE class. After each game he had some free time and we usually took him out to dinner nearby. With Kings Point being on Long Island, we started having tailgate parties where we could invite all the relatives to join us for lunch and a game. It was a practice we kept up for the entire four years that Mike played.

The first baseball season in the Spring of 1989 was a disaster because the head coach was new and he wasn't up to coaching at the college level. I approached the new coach, Charlie Pravada, who was a seasoned football and baseball coach and we both agreed that having the team practice only in the gym, all Spring, because of the cold weather, was a recipe for another losing season. I volunteered to try to put together a spring training trip to Florida to help give the team a better chance at success. When I told Tom Moran what I was trying to do, he donated one of the season boxes we had for the NY Mets games. I was able to raffle those off earning several thousand dollars. We also had a connection with George Steinbrenner, owner of the NY Yankees, who arranged room, board at a Union training center in Dania, Florida. He also provided a bus for local transportation for the team in Fort Lauderdale. Mr. Steinbrenner was also an owner of a shipyard in Tampa and had other maritime interests. The Kings Point Band usually played at the opening game in Yankee stadium each year.

We were there seven days and played six games against far superior teams however, with a new coach and spring training under their belt, the team was ready. Kings Point Baseball had its' first winning season since 1964. I kept assisting with this even after Michael graduated for several more years.

CHAPTER 37

By the late 1980's, the maritime business in the United States was changing rapidly, mostly because of the containerization of cargo. The old norm of shipping cargo in the break bulk method required longshoreman gangs of approximately 22 men per cargo hold. Containers would eventually eliminate cargo holds and would only require 7 or 8 men per shoreside crane to load and discharge the ships. The adjustment to the new norm would take years of strife and turmoil in the industry and for the weakened International Longshoreman's Association. The change did not affect the tugs handling the ships, other than the ships got bigger, requiring more powerful tugboats.

There was also a recession going on in that same period that caused a downturn in the need for oil resulting in a shutdown of many drilling rigs in the Gulf of Mexico. There were many fleets of tugs normally working the "Oil Patch" as it was known, that were now idle. This caused those tug owners to look East and North to find employment. They knew that their rates of pay for manning their tugs was about 50% less than what tug crews were earning in ports from Norfolk, VA to New York. Any effort in the past to move into the Northern ports was met with strong opposition from the ILA (Longshoremen). "If a ship is docked by non Local 333 tugs, it will not get discharged."

The ILA could no longer make that threat hold up, so we had a major dilemma that could put us out of business.

Strategy sessions happened well before the expiration of our then current labor agreement in February of 1988. Conversations with the Union leadership went nowhere. They were going to hold fast to what they currently had regarding wages, manning and work rules. Local 333 was threatening a strike before they would give up on anything. That Union also had a history of violence that we could not ignore. Al Cornette, the Union President warned me personally, "There will be blood on the string piece (waters edge)," if we attempt to implement anything other than what they have currently. We were already seeing the beginnings of what was to come. Our oil company and Public Utility customers were starting to see very cheap rates being proposed to do the same work we were doing.

A key to running a successful ship docking business in New York were the Docking Pilots and while they were employees of Moran, they were semi-autonomous, having their own billing procedures for Pilotage with the ship companies. Two months before February, I was out riding ships with our Pilots trying to let them know what was coming in the near future and trying to insure continued service. It did not go unnoticed that fully licensed and experienced Pilot, Captain Russ McVay was riding ships. Having suffered through many, some times very long strikes, with Local 333, for the first time, it was decided that we would man the vessels with other crews. We would hire people from the same labor pool that the Gulf tug companies used. This was a major decision for our Company and it was good that all of the tug/barge companies were going to fight together. We really had no other choice.

Our Curtis Bay Towing Companies were going to face the same thing with their Union, the Seafarers International Union (SIU) and their contract expired before the New York contact. Malcolm MacLeod was President of Curtis Bay Towing for all three ports and what he and his very able personnel went through, laid the groundwork for our situation.

They were successful first and there was no reason for us not to follow suit. Malcolm's crew found a man named Bill Mixon, who had a direct line to recruit hundreds of the very capable seamen. Those seamen were Cajuns for the most part and they were not going to let a little thing like a strike get in the way of them earning a living. The Cajuns were rugged, French speaking natives of the bayous in southern Louisiana. Curtis Bay did not have a Docking Pilot system like New York, so when they were ready to go with their tugs being crewed, they were short of Docking Pilots. Malcolm had asked me if I knew of anyone for those spots. It just happened that my good friend Tom Sullivan was coming home to the United States after a number of years piloting huge tankers for Esso in Saudi Arabia. Tom was hired in Philadelphia as their docking Pilot. I had a classmate from Kings Point, Steve Woyke, who had been a Panama Canal Pilot, who when offered, took the Pilot job in Hampton Roads, VA.

In New York, we had several unsuccessful negotiation sessions with the Union with all the Companies being represented by the same Law firm. The Union failed to realize that if we did nothing to meet the challenge of these southern companies, we would all be out of work. I laid out what would happen to Moran in New York as those companies would slowly pick off each segment of our business. When I announced what the pay scale was going to be, the entire union negotiating team of about 30 individuals, got up and stormed out of the room calling me every derogatory name in the book.. They refused to believe it and clearly were threatening violence as a means to their end. We hired a security company to protect our property, a company ironically named Nuckles Security. The owner of the company was Mr. Nuckles, his real name.

As replacement crews were imported, we housed them throughout New Jersey and Connecticut. We chartered several large yachts to ferry our replacement crews around, showing them the various piers that we would frequent. Tony Watt volunteered to take a chartered 50' yacht out to Bridgeport from Cos Cob to do the same thing for Connecticut ports. The boat had no radio and the night was freezing cold. The young accounting department kid he took with him to help was so seasick he was useless making a tough night for Tony.

The Diana Moran with the barge Connecticut was discharging at the Middletown Station of Connecticut Light and Power on that night in February. The bargemen finished discharging and left. The tug Engineer, before he left, filled all of the tugs ballast tanks, so the tug was stuck on the bottom. The new crew came aboard and reported that they couldn't move the tug, nor were the Captain or Mate that familiar with the Connecticut River, especially at night. This necessitated my going to Middletown where I instructed the new Engineer to pump out ballast until the tug was at the proper draft for us to get underway down the river. My memory was good from that summer I ran the Connecticut River aboard the Esso Massachusetts. The pickets were using radios to keep in contact with each other, but out of habit, they were using our same channel, so we could hear them announce their intentions. When I was done with the Connecticut River passage on the Diana, I was going to get off the tug in Essex, CT. The Union had spotters, so they knew my plans. Fortunately, I had the office call the Essex Police Department, who stationed a Sergeant on the dock. That avoided my "blood being on the stringpiece" that morning.

The New York docking Pilots went on strike with the tug crews, which was an initial setback. I knew the Sandy Hook Pilots (Bar Pilots) and worked a deal with them to do the docking/undocking as well, using our tugs for assist. Local 333 went out on strike at midnight on February 14th and we docked our first ship, using our new crews, at 0130 of the 15th. Moran's Yard in Staten Island was heavily picketed and I had an incident when I tried to enter our yard and one of the pickets took a mighty swing with a 2"x4" at the windshield of the van in which I was traveling. Fortunately, it was a Nuckles van with bulletproof glass. The man was lucky that the recoil didn't knock him out.

Strikers were dropping heavy objects off the East River bridges onto passing tug/barge units, fortunately with no injuries reported. Two, not so bright individuals, actually threw a Molotov Cocktail onto the deck of a fully loaded gasoline barge located out in Queens, NY. Had it gone off, it would have blown them and a good portion of Queens to bits. One of Turecamo's pilot's house was burned. It got so bad that we sued the Union. I had to testify in Court and the judge issued a fine on the Union for $1.00, an amount that would double every day that violence continued. It wouldn't take long for that to become a pretty significant number if it didn't cease. The Union bragged a threat that they had management's home addresses, so I and other front line people had 24 hour security at our homes. We, fortunately, had no incidents.

After several months, the striking crews started to trickle back to work and with our Pilots returning much earlier, life in the harbor began to return to normal. Our customers were happy with the reduced rates as well. Our arguments were not with the tug crews during the strike, it was the Union bosses who could not deal with what was happening throughout the maritime world. Many of the Cajun replacements wanted to stay.

They were a happy, fun group to work with and demonstrated excellent skills, very much like the men I worked with in my Chesapeake operation.

I often think back on what a monumental task it was to change out the crews on forty+ tugboats and barges, a task that involved all the people in the office as well. It was not only payroll, seamen's documentation and personnel information, but we had to make up hand books and guides for not only our Captains and Mates, but also our new engineers. Everyone was working overtime. I even brought in my high schooler Christine who helped out in the mail room. She tells a funny story about while she was in the mailroom, Tom Moran walked by and spotted her. He came into the room and sat down and chatted with her for awhile. Meanwhile, the mailroom head freaked out wondering who was this to attract the big boss into his domain.

CHAPTER 38

In the late 1980's, it became imperative that New York City had to improve their then current practices involving the treatment of sewerage. There sewerage plants were being overwhelmed, especially when the City experienced heavy rain. The rain would actually cause some raw sewerage to dump directly into the waterways. The City government came up with a plan that they thought was going to be the solution to this problem. They got permits to completely treat sewerage that would destroy bacteria and make it safe to dump 106 miles offshore in the ocean where it would further dilute the waste water on the outer boundaries of the Gulf Stream. To accomplish this task, they planned on building four 16,000 ton barges that would be shuttled to and from their plants, then out to sea to dump. We won the bid for a five year contract where they asked for a final number for the entire five year package. Our bid contained a little twist because I had a little apprehension as to whether this contract was going to last for the full five years. Environmental awareness was growing and I expressed my doubts that this contract would last for the full term. Tom Moran took that to heart and ingeniously had the bid organized so that for the last two years, it would be a break even operation and also that the five year's profit would be earned in the first three years. It was a good bet because ocean dumping stopped after three years. The reason it stopped was because a German engineering firm had invented a centrifuge that would transform sewerage into pure water and tiny bacteria free pellets that made excellent fertilizer. The city purchased four of these machines and were eventually selling fertilizer for a profit.

On March 24, 1989, the whole world and especially the United States were shocked when the tanker MT Esso Valdes, grounded on a shoal in Prince William Sound, Alaska and spilled 11,000,000 gals of crude oil into that pristine environment. We got daily TV visions of the terrible damage done to local animals, birds, fisheries and the shorelines. This disaster awakened everyone to how fragile the environment really was, especially in the pristine Northern regions. The water in Alaska is cold and doesn't support the organisms that feed on hydrocarbons like they do in places like the Gulf of Mexico. It had to be cleaned by hand and machine and that took a long time. When the mess in Prince William Sound wound up costing Esso over a billion dollars to clean up, it was going to change the industry for the better. The Oil Pollution Act of 1990 was probably one of the best laws from the Federal Government on this issue and would eventually cause all tank vessels to be built with a double hull. Groundings would damage the ship with a double hull, but would not cause a spill. The barges in our fleet were all single hull but would eventually all be double hull but, until then there were modifications that had to be made to avoid spills.

At Moran, we examined all of our practices and determined that two things that we could do was to enhance training of our crews and to better equip our units to contain and recover oil.

I knew from the beginning of my career, that if you were going to hire an assistant for yourself, make sure he or she was going to be able to take over your job, otherwise, you'll never get promoted. With this heightened awareness of Moran's responsibility to operate with the utmost care to preserve the environment, I was promoted to President, Moran Services Corporation, a position where I would have oversight and control over all the services Moran provides, for safety and environmental purposes. This was a new position with lots of responsibilities. The first order of business was to recruit every division Manager to assist in setting up training courses for our crew members, the first line of defense against accidents. It was something that developed over time. Step one was to put together a team whose sole purpose was to visit each tug in every Port to train the crew in pollution prevention of any kind, fire fighting and first aid. I became acquainted with a young fireman from Hampton Roads, VA, Bill Burket, who was adept at training for all three areas. There came a time to step it up a notch by having all of our Captains and Mates attend one week paid training sessions on Company policies regarding safety and pollution control. We held most of these sessions at facilities that had classrooms and vessel simulators for hands-on training in vessel handling. The US Merchant Marine Academy at Kings Point was home to many sessions but we also used other facilities in Florida and Maryland. All of these things we did were long before IMO (International Maritime Organization) regulations made them mandatory. As an aside, the number of our vessel accidents went down as did our insurance premiums.

The US Coast Guard facility at Yorktown, VA hosted a one week course entitled "Crisis Management," given every few years to their Captains of the Port. The participants were to address Crisis in all its forms: Fires, Explosions, Hurricanes and collisions with major spillage. They sometimes invited one or two civilians from Companies that may be important for that COTP in helping in the event of a "Crisis." I was given the honor of being invited and I thoroughly enjoyed the high pressure atmosphere of learning to deal with whatever crisis presented itself in a Port. It happened that shortly thereafter, New York harbor was selected to host a major Spill Drill, where the Captain of the Port would be given a situation with no pre-warning (grounding or collision) resulting in a very large amount of oil in the water.

A telephone call at 4:00 AM from the Captain's office alerted me that I had been asked to join him in the command center on Governor's Island and assist with allocating equipment to deal with the spill and respond to individuals with particular problems. It was exciting and the replication of a real incident had tensions high all day.

I remember that someone asked the Captain, "How many other ships are in the port that could be stained." He got very excited, standing and saying, "How am I supposed to know that? How am I going to find out?" I had Tony Watt with me who handed me a piece of paper on which our dispatchers keep a current listing of every ship in the Port. When I handed it to the Captain, he told me he wanted me there whenever a drill or a real incident might happen.

After that experience, I found myself being invited to become a Member of the Board of the New York State Oil Spill Task Force. A request to join the Board of the New Jersey State Task Force followed shortly thereafter. I was also appointed to the Regulatory Advisory Committee to the US Coast Guard in Washington to assist in the writing of the Rules to fulfill the mandates of the Oil Pollution Act of 1990.

LOWELL P. WEICKER JR.
GOVERNOR

STATE OF CONNECTICUT
EXECUTIVE CHAMBERS
HARTFORD, CONNECTICUT
06106

November 3, 1992

Mr. Russell G. McVay
8 Deerfield Road
Brookfield, Connecticut 06804

Dear Mr. McVay:

    Pursuant to Public Act 92-178, it is my pleasure and privilege to appoint you a member, representing a maritime related industry, which does not include a recreational industry, and Chairman, as one who is not a member of the Department of Transportation, of the The Connecticut Pilot Commission, to serve for a term ending July 1, 1996.

Sincerely,

LOWELL P. WEICKER, JR.
Governor

cc: Honorable Pauline R. Kezer
    Secretary of the State
cc: Honorable William E. Curry, Jr.
    Comptroller
cc: Commissioner Emil Frankel
    Department of Transportation
cc: Richard H. Strauss, Deputy Commissioner
    Bureau of Aviation and Ports
    Department of Transportation
cc: Auditors of Public Accounts
cc: Honorable Richard J. Balducci
cc: Honorable Edward C. Krawiecki, Jr.
cc: Honorable John B. Larson
cc: Honorable M. Adela Eads
cc: Honorable Cornelius O'Leary
cc: Honorable Robert F. Frankel

In the early 1990's, the Connecticut Department of Transportation decided that it would be prudent for them to follow most coastal States in having its own Connecticut State Pilot

Commission. The Commission would regulate licensed ship pilots operating in Connecticut waters. The new Rules required that all foreign ships operating in inland waters of the United States had to carry a licensed pilot. All three Ports in Connecticut, New London, New Haven and Bridgeport, were in Inland Waters. I saw an article in a local newspaper announcing the formation of such a Commission so I sent a copy of my CV to the Department of Transportation. It wasn't long before I received a letter from Governor Lowell Weicker himself, not only appointing me to be a Commissioner but he also added that I would be the Chairman of this seven person Commission. Whew! I never dreamed that my career would evolve into my being a maritime environmentalist.

A funny aside, as the new Commissioner, I thought it wise to invite those Pilots to a meeting so we could get to know one another. After introductions of my fellow Commissioners, I asked for questions from this sizable group. The first hand to go up was a fellow introducing himself as Captain Ernest McVay from Northeast Marine Pilots. Other Pilots grumbled, "Oh, they are related." I said, "I never met this man in my life."

It turns out that the Barbara McVay who I met in Point Judith, RI as a Cadet, 30 years prior, sailing in our monomoy sailboat, was his Aunt. His Grandfather was my grandfather's brother.

All of these things I wound up getting involved with, contributed to the prestige of Moran Towing Corp. being a good citizen regarding the environment.

CHAPTER 39

Moran acquired Jacobson's shipyard in 1973 and allowed it to build whatever jobs came along like tugs for Texaco, fire boats for Philadelphia and tugs for the Railroad Companies. During the 1950's they built the Eugene F. Moran and the Moira Moran. The 3,000 HP, single screw Eugenia Moran and the Grace Moran were built in the early 1970's. The last tug they built was the Harriet Moran, in 1984, after which they concentrated more on large yachts for income. The earlier tugs were tugs that I worked on as a deckhand or Mate. After the last Mr. Jacobsen no longer ran the yard, George Hosfeld was appointed as the shipyard's President. Jacobson's was known to build the highest quality vessels, a tradition that Mr. Hosfeld continued to maintain.

In 1993, Jake's, as it was called, was closed for good. The heightened awareness of our environment not only focused our efforts to make oil transportation safer, but caused us to examine all of our properties. Paint chips, sandblasting grit and anti-fouling paint just had to be removed. George Hosfeld was cautious to interact with the New York State Department of Environmental Protection Administration (EPA) and as a result, his cleanup efforts were proceeding at a snail's pace.

As Moran's Environmental Officer and because I volunteered, the cleanup of Jakobson's Shipyard became my responsibility. The mandate was "let's get this done quickly." It was going to be difficult from the get go with a 2+ hour commute from Brookfield, CT to Oyster Bay, halfway out on Long Island. For the first two weeks, I observed the operations as directed by George and my best description of his approach was "timid." Small equipment moving slowly was going to drag this out for years. The contractor, Jim Melrose, was a very decent man with good equipment and men, who agreed with my assessment and was pleased when I relieved Mr. Hosfeld of all his duties. George was of age to retire and I believe he was truly relieved to have me take over. My way of doing things was to avoid future problems with the local authorities and the regulatory bodies of the State of New York, so I went to see them both. At my visits, I outlined what we plan to do and asked for their input for their requirements and welcomed them to visit at any time to evaluate our progress. At my meeting with the State EPA, I introduce myself as being a Member of the Board of the New York State Task Force on Oil Pollution. That didn't hurt. The EPA headquarters was located at the State University (SUNY) in Port Jefferson and the open invitation to come and observe our progress, established a level of confidence with them that we were going to do the right thing.

The first thing I ordered was have an oil spill boom with a long skirt installed around the entire waterfront, to keep whatever we stirred up from going out into Oyster Bay itself.

We went from a ¼ cubic yard bucket for digging to a full cubic yard bucket, speeding things up. The spoils dug up were put into a large sealed bin to be dried, after which into sealed trucks. The polluted material would then be trucked out to Ohio to an EPA approved dumpsite. There came a time where we were running out of the material used to dry the muck. I called my friend John Mandel, the dairy farmer, who experienced rainy seasons requiring him to dry up areas where the cows couldn't walk in the mud. He solved his problem with sawdust. Armed with that knowledge, I contacted every sawmill on Long Island and they were so happy to get rid of their excess sawdust, that they trucked it to me for free. Thank you John.

There were three large steel buildings on the property that housed the shops with machines that had very good value. I placed ads in several newspapers that Jacobsen's would be selling all the equipment in our machine shops and inventory. The results were not the best but we got rid of a lot of things that we would have to pay someone to truck away. As for the steel buildings, I offered any takers to give them away to anyone who would disassemble them and remove them from the property. I had better luck selling the many sheets of high quality steel, either for money or labor to do other removals for us. The drydocks and rails were also traded for their removal. Everyplace where we dug in the yard, we did so until we found clean sand or hard pan and then we put other clean sand that we purchased from off site, to cover the yard and in the water where needed.

I invited the Chairman of the Town Council of Oyster Bay to come and witness what we were doing. They invited me to attend their full meeting to address Oyster Bay citizens and everyone seemed pleased. The local newspaper reporter was there and Moran got some very positive publicity, as well we should.

The final chapter to Jakes was that we sold the eleven acre, waterfront property, to the Town of Oyster Bay, who decided to use it as a town beach. We made it that clean.

CHAPTER 40

When I was close to finishing up at Oyster Bay, it was at that time that I heard that Tom Moran was very ill and that the Company was put up for sale. After an exhaustive search for a buyer, there was surprise to all when Tom's neighbor from across the street on Long Neck Rd. expressed interest. Paul Tregurtha was partnered with his college room mate James Barker and they owned Mormac Marine Group, operators of three ocean going American flag tankers. They also owned a Company with a fleet of ships, Interlake Steamship Co. of Cleveland, Ohio, operators of 12 dry bulk vessels servicing Great Lakes ports. My first and lasting impression of the two of them was that they were extremely knowledgeable and that you could not meet two nicer individuals.

One of the hangups to the closing was identifying what the final cost of the cleanup at Jacobson's was going to be. Fortunately, by that time the costly shipping of the sludge to the certified dump, which was the most expensive part, was finishing up. The closing went smoothly after that and of course the selling of my stock was part of it. I was no longer an owner.

I got to know Paul Tregurtha a lot better when we went

on a trip to Europe with Malcolm MacLeod who by then was President of Moran. The trip was a whirlwind, jamming a heavy schedule into three days. First, was Amsterdam, where we met with Wiismuller Tugs and Ocean Salvage Co., probably the largest tug owner in Europe. We had a very informative meeting, followed by an enjoyable demonstration of the latest tractor tug technology. From there it was off to London for a next day meeting with the West of England Club for marine insurance. We were meeting with them to introduce Paul and to educate them on the extensive preparations Moran had invested in crew training and pollution prevention. That was my part, to convince them to give us premium rates to reflect that effort. Paul was pleased that our presentation would produce positive results. I had an interesting thing happen that first evening in London while having dinner. We were in the Knightsbridge section of London, at an Italian restaurant and at the very next table was 007, Sean Connery, a very friendly sport.

The third day was a repeat, but in Oslo, meeting with the Norwegian Clubs. Then back to Connecticut. A lot got done with no wasted time or effort.

It was a sad time for both Marion and I when Tom Moran passed away. For me, he was my mentor, he was my advocate and he was my friend. Tom and Marion had a special relationship as well, as he was always happy to have her by his side when we were at the many events we attended together. I'll never forget the reception after his funeral service where we had set up a Moran tug to come into the channel going into Norwalk, CT. It was right outside their home and the tug gave a long salute with its horn. A few tears were shed with that, including my own.

At the funeral, Tom's wife Miriam, handed me a set of keys. They were keys to their sailboat and Miriam nicely said that Tom told her, "Have Russ sell it for you, you can trust him to do it right." The boat was a custom made Stevens Design sloop, 50 feet in length and valued in the $400,000 range. I did manage to sell it to a sailor living in North Carolina who wanted it delivered as part of the deal. I managed to get four Kings Point sailors to make the delivery for me.

Marion and I made many excursions to Florida on all those trips bringing the Kings Point baseball team down for spring training plus Board meetings and Captain of the Port visits. While we were on those trips there was enough free time to go exploring for potential retirement destinations. Florida was definitely high on that list. The other place high on the list was Kent Island, MD, a favorite destination of ours, since our time living at Crofton, MD, There was so much to see close by, the Chesapeake Bay for boating and blue claw crabs. We actually found a place on Kent Island on 10 acres, with a four stall horse barn plus it was on a creek with a dock. That creek had direct access to Chesapeake Bay. On one trip to that estate in the winter, the Bay was frozen, as was the creek behind the house. That cemented Florida as the leading contender. On one of our exploring trips in Florida, we went to look at Vero Beach. We quickly left after finding that Vero was not developed as yet, but on the return trip, I made a wrong turn and we found ourselves in Palm City, FL. Right in the middle of that small town was Monarch Country Club. The sales office was open so we took a tour of the community and we loved it. We actually found a beautiful 3 bedroom, 3 bath home situated on the 8th fairway of Monarch's private golf club. There was even room for Grandma Mae who was happy to go. I never had time to play golf while working but I certainly had visions of my learning how to play.

My career at Moran had plateaued with no further opportunities presenting themselves, so after 25 years of service ashore plus several years at sea and after thoughtful consultation with

Marion, I sent a letter of resignation to the Board effective September 30, 1995. The Company sponsored a wonderful retirement dinner for us that was attended by over 100 people, including our family and the many friends from both Moran and the outside organizations with whom I had the pleasure of being associated. There were some wonderful speeches and gifts to usher me off into the retirement life. Marion and I were anxious to get started on that life.

So, getting back to the title of this effort, the American dream is having the freedom to pursue your dreams of your future in a society where, if you work hard, even in the tugboat industry, it can be achieved.

Made in the USA
Las Vegas, NV
27 July 2023